A NUCLEAR DILEMMA—KOREAN WAR DEJA VU

The idea of a missile defense is not new. In 1983, then President Ronald Reagan provided the following vision to this country,

> What if free people could live secure in the knowledge that their security did not rest upon the threat of instant US retaliation to deter a Soviet attack, that we could intercept and destroy strategic ballistic missiles before they reached our own soil or that of our allies? I know this is a formidable, technical task, one that may not be accomplished before the end of this century. Yet, current technology has attained a level of sophistication where it's reasonable for us to begin this effort. It will take years, probably decades of effort on many fronts. There will be failures and setbacks, just as there will be successes and breakthroughs. And as we proceed, we must remain constant in preserving the nuclear deterrent and maintaining a solid capability for flexible response. But isn't it worth every investment necessary to free the world from the threat of nuclear war? We know it is.[1]

Since 1983, the United States has spent at least $100 billion on missile defense, and according to Lt Gen Obering, Director Missile Defense Agency in a statement provided to the Strategic Forces Subcommittee, Senate Armed Services Committee on 7 April 2005, "Nuclear-capable North Korea and nuclear-emergent Iran have shown serious interest in longer-range missiles. They underscore the severity of the proliferation problem. Our current and near-term missile defense fielding activities are a direct response to these dangers."[2]

In 1972 when the United States signed the Anti-Ballistic Missile Treaty with the Soviet Union there were approximately eight countries around the world that had ballistic missile technology while today in 2005 there are close to twenty. [3] In 2004 alone, there were over 100 foreign ballistic missile launches.[4] US intelligence experts believe that North Korea has already made several crude nuclear bombs—the only real question left is whether they have the technology to miniaturize the weapon so they are able to mount it on a ballistic missile.[5] In some minds, there's not even a question. In April 2005, the head of the US Defense Intelligence Agency, Vice Admiral Lowell Jacoby, told a senate committee hearing in Washington that the US intelligence agencies believed that North Korea had in fact been able to mate a weapon onto a ballistic missile.[6] This is not something that is "George Orwellian" or created in the minds of science fiction for in early 1998, North Korea test-fired a ballistic missile with a range of over 1000 miles that over-flew Japan and now are in the process of perfecting a missile with the capability of striking the vast majority of the US landmass.[7]

Consider this scenario: the early minutes of 25 December 2007 – Kim Jong-il had decided to do what many in the U.S government had feared for over 10 years. Under the cloak of secrecy only found in a closed, dictatorial society, Kim Jong-il had developed a new variation of the Taepo Dong missile—more than capable of reaching the heartland of the United States and delivering its 150 KT nuclear payload. With the U.S military and administration still focused in Iraq, Afghanistan and the growing global out-cry dealing with Iran's nuclear ambitions, the North Korean ruler decided that if there was ever a moment to "teach a lesson to the West" that this was the time. With the unfounded belief that no one could prove the origination of the strike, Kim Jong-il ordered his military to launch three of the Taepo Dong variants, each housing a nuclear warhead aimed at the following locations—Los Angeles CA, Omaha NE and Colorado Springs CO. To ensure complete and utter surprise, his launch order specified that the attack should take place so that the warheads would detonate in the early minutes of Christmas morning—a time that he believed that the American military, administration and people would be literally—as well as figuratively—sleeping.

With little fanfare, the North Korean darkness was suddenly illuminated as a lone Taepo Dong missile with coordinates for Offut AFB encrypted in its guidance system, bolted out of its well hidden mountain-side silo. 23 seconds later, the ground momentarily shook once again, as the second missile briefly lit the night sky as it climbed into the atmosphere on its plume of fire as it made its way towards the many military complexes located in and around Colorado Springs Colorado. Had there been a North Korean with a stopwatch in this remote part of his country, he would have noticed that there was a pause of 37 seconds before the third and final missile was slung out of its mountain-side silo, propelled towards downtown Los Angeles on its tail of fire and smoke.

Even though it was just minutes before 1 a.m. Mountain Standard Time on Christmas morning, fortunately not everyone was sleeping in the U.S. Within seconds of the first launch from the Korean peninsula, an early warning satellite in an orbit 22,300 nm above the earth's surface had alerted the operations crew as a recorded female voice broke the early morning daze—"possible missile launch—possible missile launch," and a "missile threat fan" covering the western United States is automatically displayed. Seconds after each subsequent Korean launch, the now unbelievably high tension inside the space-aged missile warning ground station located outside of Denver Colorado, became even more palpable as the woman's voice each time reported, "possible missile launch—possible missile launch."

Within seconds the crew had conducted the requisite system checks, and analyzed the data streaming from the missile warning satellites high in their orbits. Moments later the crew commander, normally a Lieutenant or Captain with as few as 24 months in the service releases a "valid missile launch" message to the Missile Warning Center, deep in the bowels of Cheyenne Mountain, buried under more than 1800 feet of granite. It is now clear that in fact there are three missiles and their intended targets are known—the United States is under attack. The Secretary of Defense and the President are woken up and alerted. Simultaneously this information is also fed into the Ground based Mid-course Defense Fire Control system located behind a heavily fortified security system in Ft Greely Alaska. Even though the North Korean missiles are only seconds out of their silos, positional, tracking and targeting data is being electronically fed into the "brains" of the "kill vehicles" mounted on top of the16 ground-based interceptors located in a nearby missile field. Within minutes, the Secretary of Defense or his designated representative authorizes a "weapons free" configuration--the battalion Fire Direction Center Director now has full authority to launch the interceptors. At precise moments, three ground based interceptors each "armed" with an exo-atmospheric kill vehicle is thrown out of its respective silo like an inverted candle, the second interceptor 23 seconds later than the first, with the third following 37 seconds later. Other than some startled Moose grazing outside the heavily fortified fence surrounding the missile field, the launches go otherwise unnoticed. Minutes later, the non-explosive exo-atmospheric kill vehicles home in on their respective nuclear warhead in their ballistic trajectories. With a closing speed of over 24,000 miles per hour, the kill vehicles—using only kinetic energy—slam into the warhead instantly creating a plasma cloud in the outer atmosphere—no debris survives to fall back to the earth. Due to the speed of the collision, a nuclear detonation was unable to occur. The proverbial bullet had hit another bullet—something that in the not too distant past had been considered impossible. In less time that it takes to have a pizza delivered to your doorstep the North Korean attack is over. For the first time since 1945, a country had attempted to use nuclear weapons. Pandora's Box had been re-opened, or had it?

In this not too far-fetched scenario, unbeknownst to the vast majority of the population, the United States had just been attacked—using the epitome of all WMD—yet there was no real visible sign that if ever occurred. The President is now forced to make a decision. Should the U.S. retaliate, and if it does, should it retaliate with nuclear weapons or do the same factors exist today that played into the ultimate decision to not use nuclear weapons during the Korean conflict during the 1950 through 1953 timeframe. Does Kim Jong-il need to worry about nuclear retaliation, or at least in this theater of operations have our nuclear weapons become the proverbial "paper tiger" sitting on the shelf with no real purpose now that the Cold War is behind us?

To get a better perspective on this situation I will take an in-depth look at the Korean War, commencing 25 June 1950 until the signing of the cease fire on 27 July 1953. Due to a number of political and military issues, the U.S. decided not to use nuclear weapons. Whether there is a direct correlation is a subject matter for another paper, however what is indisputable is that the Korean conflict became the first conflict in which the United States was not recognized as the ultimate victor. General Mark W. Clark, Commander, United Nations Forces, Korea captured his feelings in the following statement:

> …I signed a truce that suspended and—I devoutly hope—ended the fighting on that unhappy peninsula. For me it marked the end of forty years of military service. It capped my career, but it was a cap without a feather in it. In carrying out the instructions of my government, I gained the unenviable distinction of being the first United States Army commander in history to sign an armistice without victory. [8]

The author's intent is to dissect this historical example to see if any of the same political and military factors exist that could provide the reader insight into whether nuclear weapons are still a viable strategic deterrent factor in this situation. The author will then analyze unclassified nuclear strategy to get a sense if the U.S. would use nuclear weapons in retaliation for an attempted WMD attack.

Did the US try to win this war? Why did the US decide that a stalemate and an armistice were the best it could do, or wanted to do? The US had positioned itself as a "superpower" but was unwilling, or unable, to use the force necessary to bring the conflict to a successful and winning conclusion for the US. Why did the US not "pull out all its guns" to win this conflict outright? Was the truce worth 157,530 American casualties? Why didn't the US, with its nuclear superiority use atomic weapons to put an end to the war? What preparations, both diplomatically and militarily, did we make to use nuclear weapons? If the Truman administration thought it important enough to put its armed forces in harm's way, why did we not do what was necessary to win?

In regards to the Korean War, what I will show in this paper is that the US's decision to keep the Korean War limited was not for the altruistic goal of working within the United Nations charter, but simply that the US military—due to numerous reasons—was literally gutted to the point of being unable to fight a general war, especially against the likes of the Soviet Union. It was not until mid to late 1953 that the US military machine and atomic stockpile had been sufficiently rebuilt to even consider all-out war. In 1950, even with the atomic bomb, what has been dubbed the "ultimate weapon," the US chose to fight a limited war for the primary reason of self-preservation.

In an attempt to provide a better understanding of this often overlooked area, this paper will attempt to retrace the discussions and the thought making process surrounding the dilemma of nuclear weapons in the Korean War. I will analyze some of the political decisions made at the time, and the resulting impacts they had on the armed forces, leading up to and during the Korean War. I will then with some detail delve into the nuclear planning that surrounded the Korean War. Due to the nature of atomic weapons, this paper will have the majority of the focus on the political aspects surrounding their use. Finally I will end by specifically looking at this very unique scenario in which the U.S. successfully defeats a North Korean attack—an attack that very few in the U.S. even knew occurred--and then even those few who knew it occurred, never actually saw it with their own eyes. And if this were the case, whether the U.S. would retaliate with their own nuclear weapons—or whether perhaps some of the same factors that existed in the early 1950's are still with us today.

In The Beginning

> Probably one of the saddest days of my life was to walk down in that chicken-wire enclosure; they weren't even protected, what gimmicks there were...I was shocked...Actually, we had one that was probably operable when I first went off to Los Alamos; one that had a good chance of being operable...The politically significant thing is that there really were no bombs in a military sense.[9]

> - David Lilienthal, Chairman,
> Atomic Energy Commission, Jan 1947

> ...it was assumed that we had a stockpile. We not only didn't have a pile, we didn't have a stock.[10]

> - David Lilienthal, then Chairman,
> Atomic Energy Commission, 1979

> If war comes during this period...we would have a difficult time winning it.[11]

> - Joint Chiefs of Staff, 1949

By June 1950 the armed forces of the United States were in a pitiful condition. In comparison, five short years earlier the United States had spent $50 billion on its army; in 1950 it ultimately projected $13 billion.[12] In 1945, at the height of the war, there were 12 million men and women in uniform; in 1950 there were less than 600,000.[13] President Truman once remarked that everyone always wanted him to put the Russians in their rightful place, but that was hard to do when they had 260 divisions and he had one and a third.[14]

For numerous reasons that I will touch upon again later, the defense of the United States, as well as for Europe, depended upon its possession of the atomic bomb, yet in 1947 there were possibly as many as twelve available in some form or another, only 50% of those operable, however none "militarily ready" to be used.[15] Essentially still a laboratory weapon at this time, the bomb only had a "shelf life" of two days, for its batteries had to be charged 48 hours before delivery and the polonium initiator only had a half-life of 138 days.[16] The Air Force even admitted that it was not sure it could deliver one to a target if it had one to deliver. If one was able to be assembled, and the Air Force found a way to deliver it, the only real targets the Air Force knew about were the Soviet population centers. In fact the first two war plans produced by the newly formed Joint Chiefs of Staff admitted that western Europe could not be held, and that if deterrence failed, the United States could rely only on the atomic bomb—a weapon that took thirty-nine men two days to prepare for combat.[17] Depending on where the bombs were assembled, it would have required seven to nine days for three existing US atomic bomb assembly teams to load the 12 armed bombs into combat aircraft for launching at enemy targets.[18] With only twelve atomic bombs this next area was not a limiting factor, however, at that time there were only 32 B-29 aircraft, "suitably modified for carrying an atomic bomb on a combat mission," and only 12 fully qualified crews capable of making a combat drop with an atomic bomb.[19]

There was however another issue for the US Air Force and it was a significant limiting factor. The B-29, the mainstay of the atomic war plans, was a limited range bomber that could not reach many of the proposed targets within the proposed war plan. In fact, its range fell short by 300 to 500 miles.[20] The 1500 to 1700 mile range of the B-29 bomber was simply inadequate to execute a viable attack on the Soviet Union.[21]

Surprisingly enough, the unexpected Soviet explosion of a nuclear device in late August 1949 did not produce any immediate increases in the size of U.S. military expenditures. Politics and the economy were still the Truman administration's creed and would remain so until the Korean War literally forced a change.[22] Inexplicably, the budget that was submitted to Congress in January 1950 for Fiscal Year 1951 showed no reaction to the Russian detonation. In fact, the budget projected for defense was $2 billion less than the year before.[23]

It is not a stretch to say that Truman's fixation on the economy, and the resultant decision, which forced the US defense budget to originally start at $15 billion and then to be later cut to $13 billion in Fiscal Year 1950, gave considerable momentum to a nuclear-oriented defense strategy.[24] If sufficient funding was not available to build up conventional arms to a healthy and reasonable level, the only choice was to heavily rely upon nuclear weapons, which based upon their explosive power—were relatively cheap[25].

In view of the paltry conventional arms budget, the Air Force had now stepped up pressure to expand its nuclear arms capabilities. While there is no doubt that the economy was Truman's foremost passion, and thus the recipient of the vast majority of his budgets, he was uneasy over how things in the military stood—not necessarily however by the overall weakness,

6

but that he perceived that the military was growing too strong and was spending too much of his limited budgets. By the beginning of 1949, under the steady hand of Lt. Gen. Curtis E. LeMay, Commander, Strategic Air Command (SAC), Air Force nuclear-related plans and preparations were in fact showing huge improvements. There was now a combination of 120 nuclear-modified aircraft as well as six bomb assembly teams that were now trained and organized.[26] The administration remained concerned. As a result several studies were commissioned by the Joint Chiefs of Staff to evaluate the several aspects of defense, but more specifically, the growing nuclear capabilities. On 12 May, the Harmon committee submitted its report to the Joint Chiefs. Initially resisted and resented by Lemay, who had to be "cautioned" by Vandenberg—who was then the Deputy Chief of Staff of the Air Force—to cooperate, turned up somewhat awkward, but telling, findings. On one hand, the committee doubted that strategic bombing could produce the results that the Air Force claimed. There was very little doubt that the planned air campaign would produce substantial damage and casualties in the millions. On the other hand, it probably would not "bring about capitulation, destroy the roots of Communism or critically weaken the power of the Soviet leadership."[27] But at the same time, based upon the funding the services had to work with, the committee saw no other realistic choice than to use nuclear weapons and regarded them as the "only means of rapidly inflicting shock and serious damage to vital elements of the Soviet war-making capacity."[28] So simply put, the committee didn't feel reliance on nuclear weapons would achieve the administration's goals, but they had no other alternatives. Clearly the report raised serious questions about the effectiveness of the air-atomic strategy and the wisdom of solely depending on a nuclear arsenal.[29]

As for the issue concerning additional "atomic core" material, Truman reluctantly accepted the need for more nuclear weapons to augment US armed forces, and approved a substantial increase in production in the fall of 1949. Later, much to the distaste of Truman, the Korean War gave added impetus for a larger stockpile, so a second increase in atom bomb production was mandated in October 1950, and a third in January of 1952.[30]

On 23 Jan 1950, Truman finally received the briefing on the feasibility of the Air Force's strategic nuclear bombing plans that he had wanted for some time. Lt. Gen. John E. Hull, director of the Weapons Systems Evaluation Group, broke the details. The planned bombing campaign would entail enormous sacrifice and effort, with only limited results. It was expected that while 70 to 85 percent of the bombers would reach their targets, only 50 to 70 percent would make it home.[31] And while the destruction would obviously be tremendous, only one half of the Soviet's industrial facilities in the targeted areas would be permanently crippled. SAC more than likely could deliver its stockpile of now 292 atomic bombs, but would have to

7

abandon the planned follow-up conventional attacks. The truth was unfolding—the military could not deliver a devastating blow to the Soviet Union—it was as simple and ugly as that. The report went on to state that the USSR was expected to possess twenty atomic bombs as of late 1950 and would have 165 by 1953.[32] American superiority in atomic weapons was, therefore, a dwindling asset. The report went on that Moscow did not intend to unleash a general war, but if Russia ever did decide to strike, the most favorable period would be between 1951 and 1953. The President, as was the JCS, was now fully aware of the ugly situation they had created for themselves.[33]

On 14 April 1950, the National Security Council released to President Truman a report to the National Security Council by the Executive Secretary on United States Objectives and Programs for National Security (NSC-68).[34] This document established the foundations of American defense and national security policies. The basic thrust was that the Soviets had developed a workable atomic bomb and certainly would attain thermonuclear capability in a short period of time.   Based upon that premise, the Soviets would be able to launch a devastating preemptive attack against the United States by 1954. The Soviet threat to American interests, the report concluded, was "more immediate than had been previously estimated."[35] In all, NSC-68 called for more foreign economic aid, greater military assistance for the nation's allies, more investment in propaganda and information campaigns, increased military and intelligence capabilities, and a massive expansion of the nuclear stockpile.[36]

The War: 1950

> Communism was acting in Korea just as Hitler, Mussolini, and the Japanese had acted ten, fifteen, and twenty years earlier. I felt certain that if South Korea was allowed to fall Communist leaders would be emboldened to override nations closer to our own shores. If the Communists were permitted to force their way into the Republic of Korea without opposition from the free world, no small nation would have the courage to resist threats and aggression by stronger Communist neighbors. If this was allowed to go unchallenged it would mean a third world war, just as similar incidents had brought on the second world war.[37]

- President Harry Truman

> We are fighting the wrong nation. We are fighting the second team, whereas the real enemy is the Soviet Union.[38]

- Dean Acheson, Secretary of State,
Truman Administration

> ...a preventive limited war aimed at avoiding World War III.[39]

- General Omar Bradley

8

While the American nuclear monopoly had been broken shortly before the beginning of the Korean War, the atomic capabilities of the US remained vastly superior to those of the Soviet Union for the duration of the war. At the outbreak of the Korean conflict, the Soviet nuclear weapon cache consisted of between 10 to 20 bombs.[40]

It wasn't enough to merely compare the overall nuclear balance, which by the time the war started, due to the increased production, was heavily weighted in favor of the United States. The catch was that the US Government would need to ensure that its atomic stockpile would be large enough both to defeat the communist forces in Korea and to deter and possibly defeat the Soviet Union while protecting Europe at the same time. An assessment would have to be made of the usefulness of employing nuclear weapons on the battlefield, and in tactical support of ground troops in Korea. Military intelligence would have to find suitable targets as well.[41]

As stated earlier, the American stockpile was a great deal larger than that of the Soviet Union. Due to the increased attention, by 30 Jun 1950, the US arsenal included at least 292 atomic bombs and at least 22 bomb assembly teams.[42] And by the end of that same year, the number reached approximately 400.[43] The stockpile continued to increase substantially, reaching nearly 1,000 weapons as the war drew to an official stalemate in the summer of 1953.[44]

During the invasion of South Korea, and at the time of the Chinese intervention—even with the estimated 292 bombs—the American stockpile was too small for atomic weapons to be employed on the battlefield. The principal function of the US nuclear arsenal was to deter the Soviet Union from attacking the United States and the countries considered vital to American interests—primarily those in Western Europe.[45] Many in the military leadership doubted that US capabilities would be sufficient for even protecting NATO. Based upon the military strength and the air offensive as it was then envisioned, they argued that it could not prevent the Soviets from over running Western Europe. Thus any use of nuclear weapons in Korea through the end of 1952 would have left areas of vital American interest vulnerable to further communist aggression.[46]

The possibility of using nuclear weapons came up during President Truman's very first wartime meeting with his senior advisers on Sunday evening, 25 June 1950, just hours after the first indications of the attack reached the White House.[47] The president raised the issue by asking Air Force Chief of Staff Hoyt S. Vandenberg if American planes could "take out" Soviet bases near Korea. The general replied affirmatively, but said that it would require atomic bombs. That response prompted Truman to order the preparation of plans for launching an atomic attack in the event the Soviet Union entered the fighting.[48]

As MacArthur's troops were being unceremoniously manhandled in their retreat towards the sea, President Truman again met with his cabinet on 7 July and groped for some way to "let the world know we mean business."[49] Central Intelligence Agency (CIA) director Roscoe Hillenkoetter proposed seeking United Nations sanction for use of the atomic bomb.[50]

As a result of the previous day's meeting, Strategic Air Command Commander, General Curtis LeMay was ordered on 8 July, to repeat, in effect, the Berlin Blockade B-29 feint of 1948.[51] Within hours Headquarters USAF had notified Strategic Air Command to prepare two B-29 groups for England, an action that would triple the bomber force in that country. [52] To further complicate the matter, Lemay requested that many of the non-nuclear components of the atomic weapons accompany the units to England. Specifically, these were the casings of the bombs, with the high explosives and wiring, but without the fissionable nuclear cores. From Lemay's perspective, this would speed up operations in the event of war, especially with the large drain on airlift, based upon the conflict in the Far East. On 10 July the Joint Chiefs gave their formal approval, and on the 11th, President Truman gave his. Although this was officially described as merely a "training mission," the aircraft were at their newly requested and outfitted "war" bases. Perhaps not surprisingly so, one of the first rattlings of the "nuclear saber" after the start of the Korean conflict was focused not at the Far East, but towards the Soviet Union in protection of Europe.[53] Even this move, however, was somewhat of a bluff for those well informed. Strategic Air Command lacked sufficient aircraft and bombs to perform and achieve the results that the war plans called for.[54]

Though unappealing as it was to Truman, his only real available defense remained the nuclear arsenal, which remained under the control of the Atomic Energy Commission. Although preparations had been underway for sometime to train military personnel to take over these functions, the Korean War forced the issue.[55] In July 1950, the Joint Chiefs asked the President again to transfer custody of some of the nuclear weapons to the military. Truman readily agreed this time, in stark contrast to when he was earlier asked in 1948. These were the components entrusted to SAC and LeMay. As land based storage facilities became available later; additional components were also deployed to Newfoundland and Great Britain.[56]

While the England bound SAC groups were being notified, the Joint Chiefs of Staff (JCS) recommended the initiation of general war plans if the Soviet Union should actively intervene in Korea.[57] The plans called for the United States to pull out all of the troops from the Far East—to include Korea—begin mobilization, and execute the emergency war plan. Simply put, direct

Soviet involvement would prompt general war—in other words, World War III. It was precisely this that encouraged U.S. leaders to attempt to limit the scope of the Korean War. In order to prevent the expansion of fighting a war the US was not ready to prosecute and more than likely could and would not win, the Truman administration essentially funneled or "strong-armed" the US as well as the United Nations toward the concept of a limited war.[58] The free world's overall military weakness forced the leadership at that time to conserve the critical elements of what strength they did have in the dire hope of deterring the Soviet Union from more serious or threatening action.[59]

Somewhat ironically General Eisenhower, who happened to be in Washington for a routine physical examination, and who would inherit this situation some two years later, stopped at the Pentagon on 28 June.[60] He later wrote in his diary that he was astonished by the complacency and indecisiveness he found. "My whole contention," he went on in his diary, "was that an appeal to force cannot, by its nature, be a partial one. This appeal, having been made, for God's sake, get ready! Do everything possible under the law to get us going. Remember in a fight (our side) can never be too strong. I urged action in a dozen different directions...even if it finally came to the use of the A-bomb (which God forbid)."[61]

General Ridgway, who was later to take over for MacArthur, made notes on the chewing out: "General Eisenhower dropped in...[and] stated in most vigorous language and with great emphasis his feelings that we ought at once to begin partial mobilization; perhaps reinforce our European forces by a division or two; publicly increase our security measures throughout the country; at once remove the limitation placed on MacArthur to operate south of the 38th Parallel; even to consider the use of one or two atomic bombs in the Korea area, if suitable targets could be found."[62]

Generals Joe Collins and Hoyt Vandenberg, the Army and now newly promoted Air Force Chief of Staff, arrived in Tokyo on the morning of 13 July where they immediately met with General MacArthur.[63] In this meeting Vandenberg asked MacArthur about how he might cut off Chinese Communist forces if they entered the fighting. MacArthur replied that he saw "a unique use for the atomic bomb" in isolating them in North Korea. If Vandenberg would "sweeten up" the B-29 force at his disposal, the job could be done.[64] According to MacArthur's memoirs, his grand plan for defeating the North Korean People's Army was to subject North Korea to "massive air attacks," and then to "sever Korea from Manchuria by laying a field of radioactive waste—the byproducts of atomic manufacture—across all the major lines of enemy supply."[65] After his dismissal, he later remarked, "A belt of radioactive cobalt...could have been spread from wagons, carts, trucks and planes...For at least sixty years there could have been no land

11

invasion of Korea from the north."[66] In MacArthur's mind, this strategy would win the war "in a maximum of ten days."[67] The radioactive belt would not only keep the Chinese out of Korea, but would also demonstrate to China that the United States had no intention of invading. The subject was not pursued, although emergency use of the "winning weapon" was not ruled out if it became necessary to save US forces in Korea from disaster.[68] Scientists concluded, that it would have been "very difficult, very expensive and probably not very effective," albeit technically feasible.[69] The United States possessed a great deal of radioactive waste, but for a belt across Korea to have been effective, highly radioactive ingredients would be required.[70] The use of high-grade uranium would have lessened the amount available for atomic bombs, and would have slowed down the critical atomic bomb production.[71]

In an interview conducted in 1954, but not published until after his death, MacArthur stated that he had wanted to drop "between thirty and fifty atomic bombs" on enemy bases before laying the radioactive waste material across the northern edge of North Korea.[72]

When Vandenberg returned to Washington an already developing plan was modified to meet the needs of the increasingly desperate military situation. Very shortly thereafter the Chiefs added ten nuclear-configured B-29s to the SAC task force about to cross the Pacific. Doing so made perfect sense to them. It answered MacArthur's call for prepositioning nuclear strike forces close to the theater. Plus, the employment of the additional bombers implied in sorts that the JCS agreed with General MacArthur's ideas—even though he would not have operational control over the bombers—their deployment could be taken as an indication of resolve which would soften his unhappiness over other issues.[73] And so, less than three weeks after he sent nuclear-configured bombers across the Atlantic, Truman dispatched ten similar aircraft across the Pacific to Guam—where they would be available if a critical situation arose in Korea.[74]

The initial concept of using radioactive waste for a military purpose did not originate with MacArthur and, in fact, first appeared in civilian contemporary publications.[75] In early June 1950, Secretary of Defense Louis Johnson released a study of potential methods of radiological warfare, which conjectured that from the waste of atomic piles "militarily significant quantities of radiological warfare agents" could be obtained.[76] MacArthur was probably familiar with the study released by Johnson, but the idea it appears was also suggested to him by an individual from Seattle in a 1 December 1950 telegram.[77] "Why not lay down radioactive mist along Yalu. Warn Chinese this has been done. Will prove we do not intend to cross border. Will trap Reds in Korea."[78] This issue also came up at least one other time. As MacArthur was on his way back to the US after his dismissal, Congressman Albert Gore, a Democrat from Tennessee,

12

proposed to the President that "radioactive by-products" be used to contaminate a belt across "the entire peninsula of Korea."[79]

Other interesting suggestions surfaced as well. During the opening months of the war, a member of the British Parliament had suggested that the United States drop an atomic bomb on the capital of North Korea in order to bring the war to a quick end.[80] It was apparently not taken seriously by the Truman administration. However *"The Bulletin of Atomic Scientists"* quickly fired back that the statement was "obviously absurd."[81]

The attention focused on the possible use of nuclear weapons did have other effects as well. By 1951 the Atomic Energy Commission had fissionable material production in full swing, with construction of more facilities at Hanford, Washington and Oak Ridge, Tennessee in progress.[82] As the production capability increased however, so were the armed forces' requirements. Both the Air Staff and LeMay knew that the existing stockpile was increasingly inadequate for destroying the Soviet industrial base—and this unfortunately remained true through the end of 1952.[83]

The Joint Chiefs of Staff were prophetic when they stated that if war came during this period the US would have a difficult time winning it.[84] When military officers analyzed the Korean War after the fact, they found glaring weaknesses in some of the fundamental principles in the military: leadership and training.[85] Another factor was the actual combat strength of the four American divisions that were sent to Korea from Japan. With one exception, the three regiments in each division had only two-thirds of the normal infantry battalions.[86] Likewise, the artillery battalions had only two of the normal three artillery batteries.[87] Due to these shortages, the divisions averaged less than 70 percent combat effective.[88] To compound the problem, soldiers were still using out-dated WWII weapons; and possibly worse yet—weak as these four divisions were, they represented well over a quarter of the total American ground strength in the entire US arsenal.[89] What was true for the US was true for the major allies as well. The problem was that inadequate defense budgets in the pre-Korea period left them stretched too thin to cover the many risks.[90]

By the beginning of the last week in July, Washington suddenly faced circumstances that suggested that the bomb might have to be used as a deterrent to limit the scope and to possibly determine the outcome of the fighting in Korea.[91] The enemy had now squeezed American forces into a ninety-mile perimeter around Pusan. Five days later, despite General MacArthur's insistence that there be no further retreat, the North Koreans pushed the United Nations and South Korean defenders back into an area that was two-thirds its previous size.[92]

13

In supporting the decision to keep the Korean War limited, Vandenberg repeatedly put forth that the Air Force simply could not fight an expanded war in the Far East and still have forces available in the event of a general war.[93] The nation also could not afford to expend its limited, albeit growing, stock of atomic weapons in Korea or China.[94]

However, not everyone within the Air Force agreed—specifically Major General Emmett "Rosy" O'Donnell, commander of the Far East Air Force's Bomber Command.[95] "We have never been permitted to bomb what are the real strategic targets, the enemy's real sources of supply."[96] He said the strategic bombing command had been "designed to deliver the atomic offensive to the heart of the enemy," and indicated very strongly that he thought the bomb should have been used against the Chinese.[97] When General Vandenberg heard O'Donnell's statement, his curt response was "Obviously he doesn't speak for the Air Force."[98] As a direct result, on the night of 15 January 1951, Major General O'Donnell was relieved of this post and was reassigned to the Fifteenth Air Force in California.[99] A *New York Times* correspondent wrote that "General O'Donnell, one of the most outspoken proponents of strategic bombing, is leaving a command fraught with frustrations."[100]

While the war was going well, the talk of nuclear weapons was low-key to say the least. Not surprisingly then, was that the President's eagerness and desire for an expensive military build-up waned considerably when the situation improved dramatically in the early fall of 1950, corresponding with the landing at Inchon and the subsequent drive northward. However the respite was short lived as the issue of the possibility of using atomic weapons arose again in early November with the introduction of the Soviet-built MiG-15s into the theater and shortly thereafter the first evidence of Chinese intervention.[101] As the days went by and as the United Nations forces were being driven back from the Yalu, there was once again growing fear within the Truman administration and military leadership that the UN forces could be driven from the Korean Peninsula.[102]

The consensus of the Joint Chiefs of Staff was that the U.S. should try to hang on in Korea for as long as possible and attempt to establish an unbreachable line, which would encourage or even, force Beijing to negotiate.[103] Much of the continuing discussion was on where this line might be established. The State Department spokesman urged that the forces be merged to form a line across the narrow neck (roughly the Wonson-Pyongyang corridor) or, failing that, the 38th parallel.[104] However by now, MacArthur had persuaded the JCS that a line across the narrow neck was not, as General Collins put it, "a practical proposition."[105] Nor was one at the 38th parallel where defensive positions were simply unfeasible. It seemed more likely the line should be two strong, independent perimeters—one around Seoul-Inchon, the other around Hamhung-Hungnam—or in the worst case scenario, a single enclave at Pusan—again.[106]

What worried the JCS the most was the possibility that if such enclaves were established, the Communist Chinese Forces (CCF) might commit its new Soviet-supplied Air Force against American ground forces and installations.[107] If so, there was a good likelihood that the CCF could inflict devastating casualties on the closely bunched troops inside the perimeter, forcing a complete evacuation, or a Dunkirk.[108] To prevent a slaughter during the evacuation, Americans would almost certainly have to strike back at airfields in Manchuria. That action could well bring in the Soviet Air Force into the war in support of the Chinese. In that scenario the "only chance," as Collins put it, was "the use—or the threat of the use—of the A-bomb."[109] Use of the A-bomb in that context could well invite Soviet nuclear retaliation on the US itself, initiating global nuclear war—a very slippery slope, ending possibly with all out nuclear war.[110] Not the chain of events the administration wanted to occur.

On 20 November General Collins, the Army Chief of Staff, authorized a study of the use of the atomic bomb against military targets in Korea, Manchuria and China, noting that in the event of full-scale Chinese intervention, atomic weapons might be necessary to allow MacArthur to hold, and possibly even drive to the China-Manchuria border.[111]

Eight days later, Rear Admiral W.G. Lalor sent an urgent secret cable to the JCS, asking for the Joint Chiefs recommendation on "the possible use of the atomic bomb as a factor to discourage...continued intervention and/or to assist in the evacuation of UN forces from Korea."[112] Admiral Lalor asked for detailed information from the Joint Chiefs concerning the "use, timing, transportation etc." of the atomic bomb against specific targets in Korea and the "use of conventional and atomic bombs against China, with or without previous ultimatum."[113] (To highlight the sensitive nature of this communication, Lalor stated, "The only copy of this memorandum is in the possession of the Secretary, Joint Chiefs of Staff. The JCS direct that knowledge of the subject matter herein be very closely guarded.")[114]

As the grim details from the Korean Theater of operations filtered back to the American public, the pressure grew for the administration to act. On 30 November, the day after the Marines were surrounded by the Chinese at the Chosin Reservoir in Korea, Truman issued a statement that UN forces had "no intention of abandoning their mission in Korea."[115] Reporters began to question the President, leading Truman to say that the United States "will take whatever steps are necessary to meet the military situation just as we always have."[116]

A reporter followed up, "Will that include the atomic bomb?"[117]

"That includes every weapon we have," the President answered.[118]

15

Follow-up question, "Mr. President you said 'Every weapon we have.' Does that mean that there is active consideration of the use of the atomic bomb?"[119]

"There has always been active consideration of its use. I don't want to see it used. It is a terrible weapon and it should not be used on innocent men, women, children, who have nothing whatever to do with this military aggression—that happens when it's used."[120]

While there was certain reluctance on the part of many to deploy atomic weapons before the Chinese intervention, once large numbers of Chinese troops were in Korea, the Joint Strategic Planning Committee concluded that defense, rather than deterrence or compellence, was the strongest logical reason for using nuclear arms in the Far East.[121] Thus the JCS recommended that President Truman tell British Prime Minister Attlee that the United States had "no intention" of using nuclear weapons in Korea unless they should be needed to protect the evacuation of UN forces or to prevent a "major military disaster."[122]

General MacArthur had apparently studied the possible use of nuclear weapons, and was ready if the authority were ever to be given to use them. Evidently, General Vandenberg, had quickly forwarded a copy of the press release to General Stratemeyer, Commander, Far East Air Forces as well as General MacArthur. General Stratemeyer notes in his diary on 1 Dec, "Reference the [press] release, General MacArthur at 1400 hours today, in his office, stated that in a war with Communist China and if he was given the use of the atomic weapon, his targets in order of priority would be: ANTUNG, MUKDEN, PEIPING, TIENTSIN, SHANGHAI and NANKING. That if we get in the big one, his targets would be VLADIVOSTOK, KHABAROVSK, KIRIN, and a fourth one which I believe was KUYVYSHIEVKA {Capitalization in original}."[123]

On 6 December, Truman secretly endorsed the JCS recommendation that atomic bomb components be stored on the USS Franklin Roosevelt, which was patrolling the Mediterranean.[124]

It is also known that two days prior to President Truman's "revealing" press interview the JCS had ordered an additional top secret study on the employment of the bomb in the event of Soviet intervention, "to discourage such intervention and/or to assist in the evacuation of UN forces from Korea."[125] It also requested comments on the use of atomic and conventional bombs against China "with or without previous ultimatum."[126] It may have been possible that when Truman implied that the use of the bomb "was always under active consideration" he may not have unintentionally spoken. He may have in fact been warning Stalin and Mao Tse-Tung about the consequences of what may happen if there was further escalation in Korea.[127]

As the news from Korea grew worse, the administration faced tremendous pressure to prepare for the worst. The national commanders of the four largest veterans' organizations pleaded for the President to use, "such means as may be necessary" to put an end to the Communist aggression.[128] On Christmas Eve, MacArthur submitted a list of "retaliation targets" in China and Korea that would require 26 atomic bombs.[129] His plan called for four bombs to be placed on Communist forces in North Korea, four on "critical concentrations of enemy airpower," with the remaining 18 detonated on critical enemy installations and industrial concentrations.[130] Stuart Symington, Secretary of the Air Force, submitted a report to the National Security Council in January recommending tough action. He proposed evacuating Korea, attacking the Chinese mainland, and making an explicit atomic threat against the Soviets. "Atomic bombing by itself cannot win a war against Soviet Russia, but today it is the most powerful military weapon. In this world of power politics, therefore it should be further utilized in political negotiation."[131] He also sent a memo to the president that included these earlier thoughts as well as his feelings that Soviet containment was a failure. In reply, Truman used the word "malarkey" as well as several other choice adjectives to express his disgust and disagreement.[132] Truman left it clear to those in his administration that he did not agree.[133]

The War: 1951

> There is of course the school that argues for immediate use of nuclear weapons when a stalemate threatens, that talks of 'reducing the enemy to the Stone Age' by blowing his homeland to dust. This to me would be the ultimate in immorality. It is one thing to do this in retaliation, or as a measure of survival as a nation. It is quite another to initiate such an operation for less basic reasons. We have not, it may be argued, advanced too far from the jungle, over the ages; but what little advance we have made, whatever margin still exists between us and the beasts, I believe we should cling to. If we put 'victory' at any cost ahead of human decency, then I think God might well question our right to invoke His blessing on our Cause.[134]

> - General Matthew B. Ridgeway, Commander,
> United Nations Forces, Korea

> It would be militarily foolhardy to embark on a course that would require full-scale hostilities against great land armies controlled by the Peking regime, while the heart of aggressive Communist power remained untouched.[135]

> - Joint Chiefs of Staff Amendment,
> 3 January 1951

Through the last days of January and into early February, the mood began to shift in Washington and within the Truman administration. As it became increasingly evident that military disaster was not looming immediately over the horizon, many of the possibly more extreme choices—those dealing with atomic weapons—began to somewhat subside.

17

However, not everyone was willing and eager to jump off the train that easily. On 11 January 1951, Stuart Symington, former Secretary of the Air Force and now Chair of the National Security Resources Board, called for a nuclear attack on China at a secret meeting of the National Security Council.[136] He presented this plan in a secret document he submitted to Truman called NSC-100, which stated that the US military had a "prime power advantage… which every week from here will steadily decline."[137] NSC-100 called for a surprise nuclear attack on China and the "eventual disruption of the Chinese Communist Government," to be followed by an ultimatum to the Soviet Union if they made aggressive moves "in areas to be spelled out."[138] NSC-100 acknowledged that this was calling for a "political showdown" with the Soviet Union.[139]

In January 1951, the first US tests of tactical nuclear weapons took place.[140] Military planners were not slow to grasp their potential. The USAF immediately started a robust program to make its platforms capable of carrying the new tactical atomic weapons.[141] During this same period, the Joint Chiefs of Staff briefly considered the tactical use of atomic weapons to break the stalemate in Korea.[142] On 26 June 1951, General Collins submitted to the other chiefs an Army study of the possible effectiveness of atomic weapons in Korea. The conclusions of the study, endorsed by General Collins, were that no suitable targets for atomic weapons in Korea were known, but that they might be discovered by a search; that capabilities for delivering atomic weapons in Korea should be established; and that practice strikes should be undertaken, with simulated atomic weapons to provide experience to US forces in using atomic weapons in support of ground operations.[143]

The Joint Chiefs referred the matter to the Joint Strategic Plans Committee (JSPC).[144] The Committee concluded on 11 August 1951 that atomic weapons should be used tactically "if necessary to prevent disaster to our forces in the Far East," but only after full consideration of the dangers of an enlarged conflict.[145] General Collins, now reversing his stance somewhat from what he had stated earlier, now argued that that the bomb should be reserved for combat with Soviet forces and that the United States should "hold back from bombing China even if this means that our ground forces must take some punishment."[146]

The Truman administration encountered another crisis early in April 1951. While UN troops were positioned to move across the 38th Parallel in force, the Chinese appeared to be readying a massive ground offensive.[147] Added to this, Washington had indications that Moscow had moved three divisions into Manchuria and had positioned other forces for an attack on Japan. On 4 April 1951, Truman met with three of the "big four" congressional leaders, hoping to get their help in alerting Capitol Hill and the public to the dangers confronting the nation.[148] Shortly after that meeting, House Speaker Sam Rayburn warned that the country was "in greater danger of an expanded war today than…at any time since 1945."[149] As a direct result, the president decided two days later to send additional B-29s carrying *complete* atomic weapons across the Pacific.[150] That morning General Bradley had brought him the latest enemy buildup reports and the chiefs' recommendation that General MacArthur be authorized to retaliate against air bases and aircraft in Manchuria and Shantung in the event of a "major attack" on UN forces originating outside Korea.[151] General Lemay was informed of Truman's intentions on 5 April and on the 7th met with General Vandenberg, Air Force Chief of Staff to finalize the plans.[152]

The latest enemy intelligence reports were troubling. Enemy planes were stacked wingtip to wingtip on Manchurian airfields; Soviet submarines were concentrated at Vladivostok; and a sizeable Soviet force had moved south.[153] The fear was that Moscow might be about to try a one-two knock out blow, striking UN forces by air in Korea and cutting them off at sea from their Japanese bases. To check this threat, Truman decided to again use the only "arrow in his quiver"—as a result, complete nuclear weapons and SAC bombers were ordered across the Pacific. In all, nine complete atomic bombs were to be transferred to Air Force custody. [154] The following day, 7 April, the 99th Medium Bomb Wing was ordered to pick up the atomic bombs for shipment to Guam. Somewhat ironically, the movement of the atomic weapons closer to the theater of operations spelled the end of General MacArthur's military career.[155] Several days later, Truman, fed up with MacArthur's "maverick and unyielding" character called MacArthur home.[156]

Whether it was intended as a final slap in the face to MacArthur, Truman sent General Ridgeway, MacArthur's successor, a clear and concise directive giving him authority to launch atomic strikes in retaliation for any major air attack originating from beyond the Korean peninsula—authority that had never been given to MacArthur.[157] So while the weapons themselves remained on Guam, the bombers logged training flight time in preparation.[158] Early in June, in a change from their normal practice routes, and possibly as an indication to the enemy that the fighting was about to be expanded, reconnaissance aircraft over flew airfields in Manchuria and Shantung to obtain target data.[159] The pressure was steadily increasing on both sides.

Two days before the truce talks began on 8 July, there were indications that officials were thinking seriously about adopting MacArthur's ideas and bombing China if the armistice talks failed.[160] The *Washington Post* though pro-administration, verbalized the sentiment of many as the talks dragged on and the purpose of a "limited war" became less and less clear for many

19

Americans. "The Chinese should understand that if they put forth no genuine effort to bring about a cessation of hostilities in the forthcoming negotiations the resumption of the war would not be on the limited scale that has characterized it to date. The world-wide desire for a cessation of hostilities cannot be trifled with."[161]

General Matthew Ridgeway, MacArther's successor, believed that full retribution against China would not be effective unless the atomic bomb were used—however the United States must be fully prepared and understand they were most likely initiating a third world war.[162] For emergency planning purposes (code named Shakedown), SAC B-29 bombers on Okinawa would be allotted a total of twenty atomic bombs to drop on Soviet military targets in Vladivostok, Port Arthur, Darien, Sakhalin Island, and elsewhere.[163] The nuclear cores, however, were retained on American soil in the Marshall Islands or in the US itself.[164]

Therefore Ridgeway "war gamed" how, in the event of general war, some American atomic bombs in the Far East might be diverted to tactical use to assist in the preservation and evacuation of Eighth Army from Korea.[165] But ultimately Ridgeway concluded that such a course of action was not feasible. They could possibly locate a target worthy of an atomic bomb, but by the time Ridgeway got permission from President Truman to use the A-bomb and the warheads were flown from the Marshall Islands to Okinawa and the bombers were loaded and got to Korea, the target would have dispersed.[166] In reality, the red tape entailed in the tactical employment of atomic bombs would defeat any timely employment.[167] Maybe not surprisingly, General Ridgeway was not alone in this view. In August 1952, the Joint Strategic Plans Committee issued a report, JCS 1776/310, which examined options for bringing the Korean War to an end. The study concluded that nuclear weapons would have to be used against military targets in the Far East if the US government decided to pursue a clear-cut military strategy of victory.[168]

It would be inappropriate to leave the reader with only one half of the picture when discussing General Ridgeway. While General Ridgeway did "war game" the possible use of atomic weapons, he had strong views concerning their ultimate use.

> There is of course the school that argues for immediate use of nuclear weapons when a stalemate threatens, that talks of 'reducing the enemy to the Stone Age' by blowing his homeland to dust. This to me would be the ultimate in immorality. It is one thing to do this in retaliation, or as a measure of survival as a nation. It is quite another to initiate such an operation for less basic reasons. We have not, it may be argued, advanced too far from the jungle, over the ages; but what little advance we have made, whatever margin still exists between us and the beasts, I believe we should cling to. If we put "victory" at any cost ahead of human decency, then I think God might well question our right to invoke His blessing on our Cause.[169]

20

The pentagon continued to commission and churn out study after study concerning the possible use of nuclear weapons in the Korean Theater. On 5 July 1951 the Army Operations Division produced a memo giving the actions necessary to break the Korean deadlock if truce negotiations failed. It assigned a central role to the new family of atomic weapons, "In the event of a stalemate in Korea in which the Communist forces pit manpower against our technological advantages, use of the atomic bomb to increase our efficiency of killing is desirable. In the event of a general emergency including the defense of Japan, the application of the atomic bomb is essential."[170]

In September 1951, the JCS directed CINC Far East to test atomic delivery procedures by conducting simulated strikes in Korea with the coordination of SAC and CINC Pacific Command, since the Navy also had some carrier-based nuclear capability.[171] So in extreme secrecy, a series of four practice missions involving dummy bombs were carried out in Korea, code-named Operation Hudson Harbor.[172] For security the operations were conducted as conventional strikes in support of front-line troops, but they actually were conducted as close to actual nuclear procedures as possible, to include waiting three and a half-hours to get presidential permission to release the weapons for a first strike.[173] Hudson Harbor demonstrated that the evaluation of potential tactical targets was inadequate at that time, while the delay between selection and delivery was too long as well.[174] In addition, CINCFE (General Ridgeway) and SAC (General LeMay) disagreed on the best way to pick targets.[175]

The War: 1952

> We pretended we weren't there. They dressed us in Chinese uniforms. We had no documents on us—except for a small badge with Mao Tse-Tung on it.[176]

> - Soviet Air Force Colonel General Nikolai Petukhov

> …the proper approach now would be an ultimatum that could lead to all out war destroying Moscow, St Petersburg, Vladivostok, Peking, Shanghai, Port Arthur, Dairen, Odessa, Stalingrad, and every manufacturing plant in China and the Soviet Union.[177]

> - President Truman's diary, 27 January 1952

The armistice talks had been recessed for three months due to one issue—that dealing with the repatriation of the POWs—with neither side wanting to compromise on their position.[178] Because the discussions seemed to be going nowhere, the Far East Command and the Pentagon began to seriously consider a course of action if the peace talks failed completely. The Pentagon staff officers had been coming up with plan after plan ever since the talks had started running into snags, but nothing had been decided definitely. Then, on 16 October, General Clark forwarded to the Joint Chiefs his OPLAN 8-52, which was designed to turn the war around abruptly by seeking a military decision. By his own admission, Clark began planning for escalation in case Washington decided to "go for victory."[179]

OPLAN 8-52 called for a major amphibious assault, enveloping attacks to destroy the maximum number of enemy troops, airborne assaults on targets of opportunity, and—most significantly—air and naval attacks on targets in China and Manchuria and a naval blockade of China. His theory being that the communists could be encouraged to accept American peace proposals if only they were bombed enough was being carried out to its ultimate conclusion.[180]

In a letter going along with the plan, Clark pointed out that OPLAN 8-52 made no provision for the use of atomic weapons, but he strongly urged that serious consideration be given to removing the restriction on employing them.[181] Clark said he believed nuclear weapons would be essential if he was to make the most effective use of his air power against targets of opportunity and to neutralize enemy air bases in Manchuria and North China.[182] However, General Clark stated his conviction that because of the enemy's defensive positions as well as the enemy's "numerically superior" forces, any lessor action designed to obtain a military victory and achieve an armistice on US terms was not realistic.[183] He believed that his operational plan, which was now completed, would compel the enemy to seek or accept an armistice "on our terms."[184] He had not included the use of tactical nuclear weapons in his planning, but highly recommended that he be allowed to do so.[185]

While Clark's confidence was encouraged by the development of tactical atomic weapons during the summer of 1952 he was not completely won over by the concept. Even General Collins, now the Chairman of the Joint Chiefs of Staff, talked about the development of the atomic cannon and emphasized that the US would use every means to defend its troops—now sending a significantly different message than when he stated that the US should hold back from bombing China even if this meant that the ground troops must take "some punishment." It was believed tactical nukes would give the US an important technological advantage that would outweigh communist superiority in manpower. Ground offensives could now be launched at an acceptable cost, but most importantly, it would provide him a way to maintain pressure upon the enemy. Nuclear attacks could also quickly and easily destroy the MiG bases.[186]

As this was an election year, almost from the start of the 1952 presidential election campaign national policy about Korea was under intense scrutiny. On 7 November, General Collins told Clark the Chiefs were studying OPLAN 8-52 and would consider his views on the use of atomic weapons, but "our worldwide commitments for personnel and logistical support

22

are extremely heavy, and I cannot give you any indication at this time as to what action may be taken."[187] In other words, "Politically, you probably could not have chosen a more inopportune time to suggest expanding the war and the use of nuclear weapons. We will sit on this until after the new president is sworn in and has had the opportunity to develop his new policy. For the time being this plan will be shelved."

In his book, *"From the Danube to the Yalu,"* General Clark wrote in 1954, "I believe, however, that we could have obtained better truce terms quicker, shortened the war and saved lives, if we had gotten tougher faster. About this, I made specific recommendations... These included a rapid build-up of South Korean forces, the use of Chinese Nationalist divisions from Formosa in Korea, and, in the event of a decision by my government really to win the war, the use of the atomic bomb."[188]

But while General Clark was urging to take the offensive, a civilian official in Washington was counseling the outgoing Truman administration to take just the opposite course of action. Secretary of the Army Frank Pace warned the Secretary of Defense on 16 October that an "escalation of military action was irreconcilable with budgetary and manpower constraints. Any course of action involving the extensive use of UN ground troops for forcing a decision in Korea will not only prove unrealistic when measured against the availability of additional UN forces, budget requirements and our present mobilization base, but any prospect of implementing such a plan prior to 1954 is simply out of the question."[189]

When the Eisenhower administration was inaugurated in January 1953, they brought with them a similar position regarding the economy, but a significantly different policy dealing with the use of atomic weapons. Much like Truman, Eisenhower also strongly believed that economic bankruptcy could result from massive military expenditures. On the other hand, there was a need, to "maintain the great equation between military requirements and economic soundness."[190] If the United States had a technological lead in an area that would permit reductions in conventional force levels and the defense budget, then Eisenhower believed America had to be prepared to use these new weapons. He felt that the administration must remove the "moral problem and the inhibition on their use," break down the distinction between nuclear and conventional arms, where ultimately the allies and more importantly the American public think of them, "as simply another weapon in our arsenal."[191]

Eisenhower's influence on the Korean War predated his election to the presidency. As a candidate, he pledged in October 1952 to go to Korea.[192] The ultimate "success" in this trip for the Eisenhower campaign was in giving the impression of movement toward peace when, in fact, he was still very much struggling with how to put an end to the conflict. On the return trip, during a strategy session on the ship *Helena*, Eisenhower and his staff used the time to plan the broad strategy for the national security policy and contemplated substituting the use of atomic weapons for conventional ones in Korea.[193]

In December 1952, Eisenhower conferred with General MacArthur as well to hear his ideas on how to end the conflict.[194] Part of his suggestions included the US using atomic weapons and amphibious landings to clear North Korea, creating a radioactive barrier along the Yalu River and bombing Chinese bases and installations across the border if necessary.[195]

The War: 1953 and the Armistice

In January 1953, just a little over six months before the armistice was to be signed there was the growing belief in the Pentagon that the US finally possessed enough bombs to use in a war if necessary.[196] As General Bradley later recalled, by 1953 the US possessed enough atomic ordinance to "clobber the hell" out of the Chinese without reducing its capacity to wage global war.[197] In fact by May 1953, the JCS had developed their own plan of operations, which incorporated the use of the new tactical weapons against North Korea and Manchuria.[198]

Looking back, this time in history is momentous—there were finally enough atomic bombs in the American arsenal to deter a Soviet attack on the United States or on Western Europe, and to use in support of the ground combat in Korea if the need arose, as well as an administration that was outwardly willing to employ them.[199] There was one problem—by that point it was all but too late. By that time several things had transpired. First, the US as well as her allies was more eager than ever to conclude the war.[200] Secondly, as now Vice Chief of Staff of the Army General John E. Hull warned, there "were no good strategic targets within the confines of Korea itself."[201] The targets that were of any strategic value were located close to, or on the Chinese side of the Yalu river—and bombing those would invalidate the "limited war" philosophy still in place. Thirdly, the Korean War front lines had become reminiscent of WWI in the respect of trench warfare. Since early 1952, both sides "took to ground," and created extensive, fortified labyrinths from which to fight.[202] Specifically on the north side of the stalemate, there were very few large concentrations of enemy troops above ground. American tests conducted in May 1952 showed that if soldiers were dug in, and not too close to ground zero, the atomic blast would go right over them.[203] A test was carried out in which a bomb—similar in size to those dropped in Japan—was dropped in the Nevada desert. Troops had dug themselves into 4½-foot deep foxholes that were located three and a half miles from ground zero.[204] Ten seconds after the explosion, the soldiers climbed out of the foxholes, injury free. Tests performed with live animals that were placed in foxholes closer to ground zero,

24

demonstrated that they could also survive a nuclear blast without suffering any physical damage. Even the British Chiefs of Staff believed that the atomic bomb would not be effective against the Chinese, whether it was for stopping, holding up an offensive, or digging them out of the hills. But any use of nuclear weapons would make the situation more desperate by bringing in the Soviet Air Force into the war.[205] They firmly believed that the "A" bomb was the ultimate weapon and that the US should keep it in reserve as a deterrent, or for use in event of Russia launching a third world war, in other words—for the protection of Europe.[206]

Eisenhower seemed unwilling to accept the idea "that atomic weapons could not be used effectively in dislodging the enemy from their present positions in Korea," and asked about atomic penetration bombs.[207] General Hull replied that they may cause earthquakes, but in his mind it was doubtful that they would destroy many enemy personnel or much materiel.[208] Eisenhower was still apparently convinced that "it might be cheaper, dollar-wise, to use atomic weapons in Korea than to continue to use conventional weapons against the extensive dugout fortifications which honeycombed the hills where the enemy forces were then located."[209]

Eisenhower later recalled that he had been seriously thinking of the advantage of using nuclear weapons in Korea for quite some time:

> To keep the attack from becoming costly, it was clear that we would have to use atomic weapons. This necessity was suggested to me by General MacArthur while I, as President-elect, was still living in New York. The Joint Chiefs of Staff were pessimistic about the feasibility of using tactical atomic weapons on front-line positions, in view of the extensive underground fortifications which the Chinese Communists had been able to construct; but such weapons would obviously be effective for strategic targets in North Korea, Manchuria, and on the Chinese Coast...Of course, there were other problems, not the least of which would be the possibility of the Soviet Union entering the war. In nuclear warfare the Chinese Communists would have been able to do little. But we knew the Soviets had atomic weapons in quantity and estimated that they would soon explode a hydrogen device...we decided to move decisively without inhibitions in our use of weapons... We would not be limited by a worldwide gentlemen's agreement.[210]

Declassified documents show that Eisenhower's end-the-war policy was not as well planned or rational as some have claimed, or as the President had suggested. Although one of the issues in Eisenhower's campaign was that he would bring an end to the Korean War, the administration came into office with no clear cut plan, and struggled for four months before they approved the atomic contingency plans they ultimately hoped would bring the war to a close— and not an expansion to it. The ultimatum to China was the final option, tried only after Eisenhower finally accepted the hard truth that a "quick fix" atomic strategy was not likely to

25

work on the Korean battlefield. However, he would not rule out the use of atomic weapons completely. [211]

On 11 February 1953, just a month after the inauguration, General Omar Bradley at a secret meeting of the National Security Council, called attention to the Kaesong area, which was 28 square miles and "was now chock full of troops and materiel."[212] The minutes of that secret meeting show that Eisenhower:

> Then expressed the view that we should consider the use of tactical atomic weapons on the Kaesong area, which provided a good target for this type of weapon. In any case, the President added, we could not go on the way we were indefinitely. Gen Bradley thought it desirable to begin talking with our allies regarding an end of the (Kaesong) sanctuary, but thought it unwise to broach the subject yet of possible use of atomic weapons. Secretary Dulles discussed the moral problem and the inhibitions on the use of the A-bomb, and the Soviet success to date in setting atomic weapons apart from all other weapons as being in a special category. It was his opinion that we should try to break down this false distinction.[213]

An example of the how the Eisenhower administration sought to find its way during the early portion of its presidency is seen in the following example. In addition to his military advisors, Eisenhower also discussed possible atomic strategies involving Korea with a group of civilian consultants, most of them high-ranking businessmen from the international wing of the Republican Party. [214] At a special NSC meeting that they attended on 31 March 1953, Eisenhower suggested the use of atomic weapons to achieve a substantial victory in Korea and to obtain a truce line at the "waist" of the peninsula.[215] It was then suggested that "a massive victory in Korea" be the goal versus establishing the truce line. One of the consultants, David Robertson, president of the Brotherhood of Locomotive Firemen and Engineers, voiced the opinion that the American people would support such an "all-out effort in Korea," if the end goal was total victory. [216] Deane W. Malott, president of Cornell University, suggested that perhaps the United States should drop "a couple of atomic weapons in Korea" to help break down "public hysteria" over their use.[217] Eisenhower stated however that the fears of America's European allies that they might become an atomic battleground in retaliation ruled out that tactic for the present time.[218]

With regards to the use of atomic weapons, the JCS listed the possible advantages and disadvantages and presented the following conclusion:

> The efficacy of atomic weapons in achieving greater results at less cost of effort in furtherance of US objectives in connection with Korea point to the desirability of re-evaluating the policy which now restricts the use of atomic weapons in the Far East. In view of the extensive implications of developing an effective conventional capability in the Far East, the timely use of atomic weapons should

26

be considered against military targets affecting operations in Korea, and operationally planned as an adjunct to any possible military course of action involving direct action against Communist China and Manchuria.[219]

The report went on to state that the use of nuclear weapons would prove advantageous if it could bring about a favorable settlement of the Korean War without causing hostilities to spread to China or to the Soviet Union.[220] But the study also pointed out a dilemma concerning atomic weapons that had faced the previous decision-makers as well. If their use were effective, the credibility of nuclear weapons both as a deterrent and actual battlefield weapon would be greatly enhanced. On the other hand, the use of atomic bombs could prove to be disastrous if their use were ineffective. If they failed to achieve decisive results in Korea, the value of nuclear weapons would be substantially reduced. As a result, the perception would grow that the atomic bomb offered little help in repelling aggression and its credibility, as a deterrent would significantly decline.[221] The allies in Western Europe were obviously greatly concerned with this factor as they depended upon a nuclear guarantee to prevent an attack by the Soviet Union.[222] Furthermore, any decision to use nuclear weapons would risk the loss of support from American allies if they did not concur with the decision to use them—and by late 1952, early 1953—no ally on record supported escalating the conflict nor the introduction of atomic weapons in the Far East. Eisenhower was certainly aware of the European views, but was not about to let his hands be tied. He believed that decisive leadership was called for, and that if American efforts proved successful, the United Nations would ultimately applaud their fortitude. The Joint Chiefs unanimously warned as well that no escalation on the part of the United States "should be undertaken without a concurrent decision to employ atomic weapons on a sufficiently large scale to ensure success."[223] The Joint Chiefs concurred on this position and General Omar Bradley, Chairman of the Joint Chiefs, relayed their position and recommendation to President Eisenhower, "It is the view of the Joint Chiefs of Staff that the necessary air, naval, and ground operations, including extensive strategic and tactical use of atomic bombs be undertaken so as to obtain maximum surprise and maximum impact" on the enemy, both militarily and psychologically.[224]

In the end Eisenhower agreed with the Joint Chiefs and at the NSC meeting on 20 May decided to undertake an offensive to the waist of Korea, accompanied by air and naval attacks on the Chinese mainland, and possibly most importantly, *the use of nuclear weapons would support all these actions.*[225] He believed that in order "to keep the attack from becoming overly costly, it was clear that we would have to use atomic weapons."[226] He also believed that the decision would "depend on military judgment as to the advantage of their use on military targets."[227] Eisenhower realized that "there were not many good tactical targets," but he felt it would be worth the "cost" if nuclear weapons would help defeat the communist forces and would also have the added benefit of lowering the number of casualties which the US troops would suffer in their drive to the waist of Korea.[228] He felt strongly that "somehow or other the taboo which surrounds the use of atomic weapons would have to be destroyed."[229] Eisenhower reiterated this belief a few months later, saying "he had reached the point of being convinced that we have got to consider the atomic bomb as simply another weapon in our arsenal."[230]

It was during this 20 May meeting that General Bradley briefed the NSC on the advice that the JCS had given the President. Eisenhower summarized the JCS view concisely: "to win the conflict, the United States must carry the war beyond the Korean peninsula with atomic weapons."[231] Eisenhower suggested that the quicker the United States could mount the operation the less likely a Soviet intervention and a wider war. To counter the expected uproar from American allies, he proposed gradually introducing the idea of deploying atomic weapons to hopefully make the decision more palatable. For merely planning purposes, the president suggested a potential D-day sometime in May 1954—12 months in the future—sufficient time to build up forces and ready the nuclear weapons.[232]

Eisenhower however, felt that certain actions needed to be accomplished before launching the attack. Eisenhower believed that the previous administration had sent mixed signals to China and the Soviet Union leading up to and including 1950 concerning the US commitment to Korea and on the possible use of atomic weapons during the conflict. Eisenhower decided that it was best to explain to Beijing that the United States was prepared to use atomic weapons to end the war if a satisfactory armistice appeared unworkable. That way his "cards" would be on the table, and neither side could claim they were not aware what the other was thinking. The exact timing of these signals to China is less than clear. An Eisenhower aide, although one not directly associated with the decisions in Korea, seems to place the first indication of the "atomic signal" to the Chinese prior to the death of Stalin—while other resources counter that that is highly unlikely. The first clear evidence comes to light in May. Whatever the exact date, Eisenhower and the administration agreed to pass three messages to the Chinese—the "gentlemen's agreement" that the UN force would not cross the Yalu, would not bomb bridges on the river, and would not use atomic weapons, were now all revoked. It would now be a new ballgame with new rules. And the UN was going to use new "bats" this time.[233]

The Eisenhower administration apparently sent covert messages to Beijing though a neutral government and through lower officials at the Panmunjom armistice talks.[234]

28

Eisenhower had hoped that it would add sufficient momentum to the negotiating process to ensure a settlement. Whether it was by sheer luck, or the uncertainty of the decision he had made, the president approved the delivery of the atomic ultimatum only after China and North Korea were beginning to show signs of concessions at Panmunjom.[235] According to Eisenhower's later recollections, the Chinese were told "that they must agree to an armistice quickly, since he [Eisenhower] planned to remove the restrictions of area and weapons if the war had to be continued."[236] There is considerable uncertainty whether or not Beijing ever received these threats, however the Chinese are unlikely to ever admit that atomic blackmail compelled them to the peace table even if it had. Whether Eisenhower's threat broke through the logjam is impossible to know; though there are strong indications that it did, or at least partially contributed. What may have been an equal, if not more significant incident is that on 5 March 1953 Stalin died. And then quite by surprise, at the end of that very month, Chinese Foreign Minister Zhou Enlai accepted an International Red Cross proposal for the unconditional exchange of sick and wounded prisoners of war that wished to be returned to their countries. What exact event, or chain of events, brought the Chinese back to the table is not important. The critical fact here is that a nuclear threat possibly played a role in bringing a conclusion to the Korean War.[237]

This is what is known with certainty. The ultimatum was delivered two days after the Eisenhower administration had approved a contingency plan for atomic warfare against China and three days before UN negotiators presented their final proposal at Panmunjom.[238]

But discussions of the possible uses of the atomic bomb were not done. There appears to be some evidence of an almost subconscious desire by Eisenhower or his administration for one final try for an easy, and possible spectacular solution to the Korean deadlock. On 6 May, President Eisenhower suggested at the end of the National Security Council meeting, that tactical atomic weapons be employed against four North Korean airfields that were being re-supplied with planes.[239] The UN force already was attacking them with conventional bombs, the president noted, and such a move would "test the effectiveness of an atomic bomb."[240] He concluded, "we have got to consider the atomic bomb as simply another weapon in our arsenal."[241] The Chairman of the Joint Chiefs noted that airfields were not good targets for atomic weapons, and that particular issue was dropped at that point.[242]

The much sought after armistice was signed two months later. The Eisenhower Administration had demonstrated its resolve, for it had stood ready to risk numerous US casualties on the battlefield and considerable criticism from America's allies and, in the end, was prepared to carry out the nuclear threat—only now the US was finally in a position to back

29

up the threat. Eisenhower was true to his word and had made certain that the military was in a position to be able to carry out the threat if ordered to do so. At the Bermuda Summit in December of 1953, after the armistice was signed, Dulles admitted that "we had already sent the means to the theater for delivering atomic weapons."[243] Sherman Adams, the Assistant to the President, later confirmed during the spring of 1953, that the United States had "moved atomic missiles to Okinawa."[244]

End of the conflict

> It is the view of the Joint Chiefs of Staff that the necessary air, naval, and ground operations, including extensive strategic and tactical use of atomic bombs be undertaken so as to obtain maximum surprise and maximum impact…[245]

> - Joint Chiefs of Staff
> Recommendation to President Eisenhower

In retrospect, President Eisenhower threatened to use nuclear weapons because he considered it the only way in which a relatively "quick" settlement to the Korean War could be obtained on his terms. Possibly more importantly, he now had something that Truman did not have until literally his very last days in office—a nuclear stockpile large enough to use against both China and the Soviet Union. The long stalemate on the battlefront and the breakdown of negotiations had also demonstrated that greater military pressure had to be placed on China. The enhanced US atomic capabilities finally available in late 1952, had provided the Truman administration with the means to decisively threaten the Chinese, but he and his administration were not about to undertake any major new initiatives with only a few days remaining in office. Further actions would have to wait for the Eisenhower.[246]

By threatening "massive retaliation" to end the war, Eisenhower took and supported the concept in which he had always wanted to believe in. Plus, he found atomic weapons attractive on the grounds of cost. When he had the opportunity to fully scrutinize the entire scope of NSC-68, President Eisenhower firmly believed that the spending called for in that plan would simply bankrupt the United States—"It would be impossible…to maintain military commitments around the world…did we not possess atomic weapons and the will to use them."[247]

Finally, the United States had sought all along to prevent the success of this perceived Communist attempt to expand by the use of force, in the belief that allowing the Soviets to succeed in Korea would encourage them to try it elsewhere. General Omar Bradley alluded to this thinking at the MacArthur hearings in describing Korea as "a preventive limited war aim at avoiding World War III."[248] A war that the Truman administration knew they were in no condition to win. The defense of Korea was partly motivated as well by the feeling that the action was necessary to convince the Europeans that the United States would come to their aid, if and when necessary. The Truman administration had always been concerned about committing its relatively small military force, leaving itself exposed to Stalin's aggression elsewhere in Europe. In fact, during the later stages of the Korean War when the services were finally starting the see the fruits of larger defense budgets, the vast majority of the buildup was funneled to Europe— not to the war effort that was continuing in Korea.[249]

Though the United States could have attacked the Soviet Union with its very limited stockpile of atomic weapons, it could not have prevented a determined Soviet ground attack in Western Europe.[250] All along, the United States was on guard that the Korean War not be allowed to drag them into a situation that would force them to use those military capabilities which were considered an important deterrent to general war. In Korea, the United States was only employing those troops and materiel that it felt was absolutely necessary to deter general war. At the MacArthur hearings, General Vandenberg rejected a senator's suggestion that the United States should commit a major part of the American Air Force and land forces to the Korean War effort.[251] Instead he argued that the United States must get a cease fire "without endangering that one potential that we have which has kept the peace so far, which is the United States Air Force; which, if utilized in a manner to do what you are suggesting, would, because of attrition and because the size of the Air Force is such and the size of the air force industry is such that we could not still be that deterrent to (general) war which we are today." [252]

American military leaders in Washington, and elsewhere knew the truth as well. "It would be militarily foolhardy," stated a Joint Chiefs of Staff amendment on 3 January 1951 to a State Department circular intended for diplomatic dissemination, "to embark on a course that would require full-scale hostilities against great land armies controlled by the Peking regime, while the heart of aggressive Communist power remained untouched."[253]

In a hearing before the Committee on Armed Services and Foreign Relations, General Vandenberg reiterated this point concerning the weak state of the military in his testimony, "Starting from a forty-odd-group Air Force, the aircraft industry is unable until almost 1953 to do much of a job toward supplying the airplanes that we would lose in war against any major opposition."[254]

We had found ourselves in a catch-22 situation. Desperately needing to preclude the start of a general war with the Soviet Union and/or China, we actively continued to develop plans for the use of nuclear weapons in the Far East to both protect our troops if the need arose, or possibly even put an end to the conflict on favorable terms for the United Nations. Yet it was the use of these very weapons that had the very real potential of starting general war—the war we were not ready or prepared to fight and win. And so despite the lamentable condition of our armed forces leading up to, and during at least the early years of the Korean war, we continued to actively develop plans for the use of nuclear weapons in this conflict—for we felt we had no other choice.

I contend there were at least six reasons that the United States—a self-proclaimed "superpower" at the time—did not use its atomic weapons to potentially create a more favorable end to the war.   First, the Joint Chiefs of Staff and the civilian policy makers continued to feel that the war in Korea was basically a Soviet feint. There was, therefore, a strong case for conserving the then relatively limited stockpile of atomic weapons for the general war which, they strongly believed, would come in Europe. There was a strong fear that this was a deliberate attempt on behalf of the Russians to get the United States to exhaust its nuclear stockpile so that they could later attack in Europe with no fear of retribution.

Secondly, our nuclear policy was also affected by the feelings that there were no suitable targets for atomic weapons in Korea. This added to the fact that the Korean War front lines had become reminiscent of WWI in respect to trench warfare. The impact of this view was considerable and it reflected an unfortunate uninformed attitude about the possible uses of atomic weapons. Policy makers came to think, for example, that nuclear weapons were of little use against bridges based upon examples in Hiroshima, where they remained standing after the blast. There was also a significant concern that the real benefit of nuclear weapons would not be achieved due to the dampening effect and containment caused by the hilly and mountainous North Korean terrain.

Thirdly, American allies, specifically the British, were strongly and emotionally opposed to the use of atomic weapons in the Korean War. While there is no conclusive evidence, this opposition may have stemmed from the fear that the US may have become embroiled in the Far East, at the expense of the protection of Europe. This pressure from allies strengthened Truman and his administration's moral doubts about again using these weapons.

Fourthly, I believe historical evidence shows that we chose to not use atomic weapons in the Korean War because of the fear of retaliation by the Soviets, as well as potentially opening the war to the Chineese. An atomic bomb attack on Pusan or against the American build-up in Japan would have had a devastating affect in the US as well as overseas in Europe.

Fifthly, Truman's personal feelings concerning nuclear weapons played a major role in his reluctance to use the ultimate weapon at his disposal. On 19 January 1953, as recorded in his secretary's files, President Truman stated that "The Atomic bomb…is far worse than gas and

32

biological warfare because it affects the civilian population and murders them by the wholesale."[255]

Lastly, despite the considerable political and military preparations to use nuclear weapons in Korea, the author contends we were never in a strong enough position militarily to use atomic weapons to end the conflict in our favor until early in 1953, and by that point the armistice was on the horizon, the US public as well as the allies could no longer stomach the war. While this runs counter to the whole notion of the US "superpower" status, the most honest reason the U.S. sought to keep the Korean War a "limited war" was the stark realization that the U.S. was not in a position to win a general war against Stalin, nor Mao Tse-tung.

A Return to the Original Question

So once again I pose the original dilemma: in a scenario in which we are able to successfully thwart a North Korean nuclear ballistic missile attack, would we retaliate with an atomic weapon? Should we? Which, if any of the same reasons that precluded their use during the Korean War, still exist today?

While it is well documented that the United States' stockpile of nuclear weapons was paltry, if not nearly non-existent leading up to, and during much of the Korean War, the same cannot be said today. While the exact numbers are classified, there are still more than 30,000 nuclear weapons in the world today, with roughly half of those belonging to the United States.[256] What may be surprising was that the U.S. was in fact without a capability to produce nuclear weapon "pits" for over 14 years—the key fission component of a nuclear weapon—without which it is impossible to initiate a nuclear reaction.[257] So while not in the dire straights we were in during the 1950's, in 2003 the U.S., somewhat ignominiously, reestablished its ability to make "stockpile grade" cores for its nuclear weapon stockpiles.[258] And once again, the U.S. became a nuclear power capable of producing nuclear weapons—after a little known 14 year hiatus.

The second issue that I addressed in the earlier history of the Korean War, was the overwhelming consensus that there were no suitable targets for atomic weapons—targets that if destroyed would have a devastating impact upon the enemy. A corollary issue that I believe is a follow-on of the first, is the underlying fear that if nuclear weapons were used, and they did not have the desired result of turning the war in the favor of the U.S., nuclear weapons would no longer be a viable deterrent force—a risk the U.S. could not afford to take. Many of these misperceptions I believe are attributed to the fact that very little research had been conducted to determine the overall effects of nuclear weapons, and that the first real "tests" to determine their explosive capability occurred in operational drops over the Japanese cities of Hiroshima and

Nagasaki. The earlier tests conducted in the Bikini Atoll and in the desert were for one reason and one reason only—to verify that the designers had in fact created a core which would go critical, create nuclear fission, and be reliable. That is not the case today—it is just the opposite. It should come as no surprise the U.S. has conducted a whole host of research to better understand the capabilities of nuclear weapons over the past 50-plus years. One such example that I'll refer to extensively in this paper is a study conducted by the RAND institution, sponsored by the United States Air Force in 2000—which after a considerable governmental clearance and public release review, was formally released in 2003.[259] While addressing numerous aspects regarding the potential use of nuclear weapons, of particular interest that I'll reference and that I feel are germane to this paper are the four specific cases in which scientific comparisons were made between the use of nuclear and conventional weapons. The four cases covered were: ability to stop an invading army, ability to destroy a hardened bunker containing WMD, ability to destroy deeply buried facilities, and finally in defense of ballistic missiles. (It is this last case that I will not specifically address as I assumed in this research paper that the U.S. has already fielded a non-nuclear ballistic missile kinetic kill vehicle.) The initial results of the study are not necessarily surprising. In every instance, nuclear weapons were as effective, if not more, in accomplishing the desired goal.[260]

What many may find more surprising is what the report went on to say. The report added that with the proliferation and availability of precision-guided weapons and other conventional weapon advances that in almost all situations—with the notable exception of deeply buried targets—conventional precision guided weapons could achieve the desired effect as well.[261] In fact there were certain advantages in using conventional weapons over nuclear weapons, for example, the aircraft delivering the nuclear weapon(s) must be at a safe distance to preclude blast damage—which means a very high altitude, or have the ability to quickly depart the area.[262] Another interesting point that the authors of the RAND study bring up, is that the use of conventional weapons for any of these purposes—for example to stop an advancing army—does away with all the additional "baggage associated with nuclear weapons—e.g., release authority, nuclear training for air crews, collateral damage, diplomatic impact."[263]

One other very important fact this RAND report concludes, is that geography—the very issue that had been viewed as detrimental during the Korean War—could actually help reduce the very real potential dilemma of nuclear fallout, as well as additional collateral damage.[264]

The third issue I posited for not using nuclear weapons during the Korean War was that the allies strongly and emotionally opposed the use of nuclear weapons. While it is admittedly extremely difficult to judge the international reaction to an event of this nature, there are some gauges that we can apply to possibly get some sense as to the international perspective. For example on 19 January 2006, French president Jacques Chirac slightly broadened his country's nuclear deterrence policy. In his recent speech, Chirac stated, "The leaders of those nations, who would resort to terrorist means against us, as well as those who may consider the use, in any way, of weapons of mass destruction, must understand that they will expose themselves to a firm and adequate response on our part. That response may be conventional, but it can also be another kind."[265] This warning is in fact very similar to those given by Secretary of Defense Cheney and then U.S. president George H. Bush prior to the first Gulf War in 1991 when he stated, "it should be clear to Saddam Hussein that we have a wide range of military capabilities that will let us respond with overwhelming force and extract a very high price should he be foolish enough to use chemical weapons on United States forces."[266] It is also reported in a variety of resources that the American government provided a private warning to Iraq that "in the event of a first use of a weapon of mass destruction by Iraq, the United States reserved the right to use any form of retaliation (presumably up to and including nuclear weapons)."[267] Not more than 12 years later, President George W. Bush, according to leaked administration documents, "signed a document stating that he reserves the right to respond with 'overwhelming force—including nuclear weapons' if Saddam Hussein used chemical or biological arms to attack American troops. The classified national security directive replaces the usual vague phrase 'all of our options' used in public documents, with the specific threat of 'nuclear weapons.'"[268]

To provide some insight into the British point of view on the use of nuclear weapons, on 15 November 2000, Duncan Menzies, Advocate Deputate for the Crown, and speaking on behalf of the UK, stated the following,

> ... if the nuclear power aggressor was threatening the territorial integrity of a non-nuclear victim state, let's take it, the example of China being a nuclear power threatening New Zealand, a non-nuclear power, with a battle fleet armed with nuclear missiles which it was stating it was about to fire at New Zealand and which battle fleet was in the Pacific, approaching the point at which the state of New Zealand was in range of its nuclear missiles, in such a situation I submit that it would be consistent with international law, including humanitarian laws applicable to armed conflict, for another nuclear power to use nuclear force against that battle fleet...[269]

While I would be the first to agree that it is impossible to know exactly how another sovereign country would react to the situation provided in this very unique and narrow scenario, the statements provided above by leaders in these allied nuclear powers hopefully provide some insight into their perception of the use of nuclear weapons—and at a minimum, at least do not appear to completely negate the potential use of this class of weapons.

Our fourth area of comparison was that there was a very real fear of Soviet retaliation had the U.S. used nuclear weapons to attempt to bring the Korean conflict to a more desirable end state than the negotiated settlement we ultimately accepted. There is very little reason to believe given the current geo-political situation in the world today, that Russia would begin "rattling their sabers" especially if all intelligence pointed to North Korea as being the aggressors. The same may not necessarily hold true for China. In a report written by the Congressional Research Office in July 2003 for Congress entitled, "*North Korean Crisis: Possible Military Options,*" it states, "In considering a war option, certain assumptions and risks would need to be assessed. First, international support for the war would be desirable, given U.S. reliance on global communications and transport; China's reaction would be key—at the minimum it would have to be neutral."[270] Another potential threat that the administration may have to consider prior to using nuclear weapons is one from North Korea itself. While there has been a considerable amount of rhetoric from North Korean leadership, one particular issue that has to be considered—if only just because the significant implications—is that North Korea has stated that they would "respond to any U.S. military action against it by smuggling nuclear bombs into the United States and detonating them covertly even after having 'lost' a war."[271]

The fifth reason given by the author as rationale for not using nuclear weapons during the Korean War is that of Truman's personal feelings about these types of weapons. Just as it's difficult to assess how another country will react to a given situation, it is equally impossible to judge with any degree of certainty how any administration will react unless they have already come out with a public statement. And even in those instances where an administration has come forth with a "guarantee," any number of nuances may exist at any given time, which would cause them to change their minds or make a different decision. For example, President Eisenhower having lived through the horrors of World War II is quoted as saying to his advisors who were advocating the development of a new nuclear weapon which would allow the United States to win a nuclear exchange, "You can't have this type of war. There just aren't enough bulldozers to scrape the bodies off the streets."[272] This is almost diametrically opposed to his earlier positions in which Eisenhower threatened the use of nuclear weapons as he felt they were the only way to quickly resolve the conflict in the U.S.'s favor. Taking a very different approach is Margaret Thatcher, the long time British Prime Minister who stated to a special joint session of the U.S. Congress on 20 February 1985, "Be careful above all things not to let go of the atomic weapons until you are sure, and more than sure, that other means of preserving the peace are in your hands."[273]

Not only do personal feelings come into play in a decision of this magnitude, but possibly of equal importance and perhaps greater is that of maintaining the moral high ground as well as complying with the principle of proportionality—simply the fear that the damage caused by the nuclear weapon would be out of proportion to any legitimate political or military end.[274] As an obvious extension to this "moral high ground" dilemma, is the will of the American people. In this very narrowly constructed North Korean scenario, would, and could the U.S. maintain the moral high ground by retaliating with nuclear weapons when the U.S. had sustained no visible damage upon the homeland, and no one had been injured? Would the U.S. maintain the support of the international community when there was no "smoking gun" as there was when the Japanese bombed Pearl Harbor, and then again with the images of the crumbling World Trade Center towers being played over and over again on our televisions? In both of those instances, something tangible had been destroyed. Innocent people had been brutally attacked—without provocation and without warning. The American people, as well as the administration wanted revenge. The international community felt our pain, and thus the vast majority supported our actions in Afghanistan.

But now imagine for a moment, waking up one morning and hearing something like the following on the morning news, *"…the country has been attacked during the early morning hours by three North Korean missiles. The intelligence communities—while not 100% percent certain—believe that the missiles were armed with nuclear warheads."* The report goes on to say, *"The oft-aligned ballistic missile defense system was worth every dollar, as it miraculously intercepted and destroyed each warhead approximately 80 miles above the Pacific Ocean. Not even a single piece of debris survived the impact; moreover there was no damage and no fatalities. The president and his administration are looking at what should be the next course of action."*

It is easy to find those on both sides of the aisle with very firm beliefs as to the appropriate use of nuclear weapons—when they should, and should not be used. For example, retired Admiral Stansfield Turner in an article published in the NWC Review stated, "The nation needs to be brought to understand that nuclear weapons are generically different from conventional weapons. They are too powerful to be used for anything but deterrence or—God help us— retaliation."[275] Senator Joseph Biden, Jr. from the state of Delaware echoes those feelings almost verbatim as he states, "Nuclear weapons are weapons of retaliation or last resort. They are not handy military tools, and we must not allow ourselves to think of them in that way."[276] However for the first time in history, the current administration has taken that very approach as it has put forth a new nuclear doctrine as it released the Nuclear Posture Review in January 2002, followed by the National Security Presidential Directive 17, in September 2004. These documents suggest that this administration is possibly moving away from deterrence as the sole purpose of nuclear weapons, and more to a true warfighting—potentially to a preemptive—role.[277] Is it more than just posturing—perhaps a new form of "Post 9-11" deterrence? According to Robert G. Spulak, Jr., in his article "The Case in Favor of US Nuclear Weapons," he states that, "Credible nuclear deterrence is robust, not delicate. Policies and actions that establish credibility couple with our nuclear arsenal to create the possibility that in a war with the United States an enemy may face a risk of annihilation. A potential enemy need not even be very rational to be deterred from actions that ensure his own destruction."[278] Colin Powell and General Lemay believed as well that "once you make a decision to use military force to solve your problem, then you ought to use it and use an overwhelming military force…And you save resources, you save lives—not only your own but the enemy's too." [279] This also coincides with what Dr Yarger stated is one of the most important considerations for our strategy and policy, that being that we have the national will, and the full means to carry out our "threats" or our stated actions.[280] I believe it is reasonably clear that this administration has the will and the full means to make good on this "new" nuclear warfighting concept.

But does having the "will and means" to use this new warfighting concept sufficient? Does this by itself answer the question of whether we would actually resort to the use of WMD? I contend that it does not.

> …there is the question of whether a national policy of deterrence by threat of punishment will continue to be politically sustainable in the future. The punishment inflicted on Yugoslavia by precision conventional bombing during the Kosovo campaign to coerce Serbian acquiescence to NATO's conditions for peace undoubtedly caused some Americans to have moral qualms about inflicting even that degree of pain on civilian populations. The sustained economic sanctions on Iraq appear to have done much more damage to Iraqi civilians than to Saddam Hussein's government. With that sort of recent experience, will the American public continue to support a policy that threatens vastly greater damage?[281]

The last comparison that this paper will analyze is the claim that the U.S was not in a strong enough position militarily in the early 1950s while involved in the Korean War to use nuclear weapons. The thought behind this being that if nuclear weapons were used, that it would raise the conflict to a new level—one that the US military was not prepared to fight in its current state. The question is this; could the same argument be made today using this scenario? Without having to go very far, one can find almost eerie similarities. In the Congressional Research Service report to Congress detailing possible military options in North Korea, it emphatically states that, "…timing is a problem—due to heavy commitments in Iraq

38

and many other places, the U.S. Army is currently stretched very thin, and would find it difficult to contribute the major ground forces needed. To sustain such an operation, it is likely that many Army National Guard and Army Reserve units not already on active duty would have to be mobilized, as well as considerable numbers of individual reservists to fill out units and replace casualties."[282] And in separate congressional testimony, the Army, Air Force, and Navy have all stated that recapitalization of their forces is essential.

Citing another example, in January 2006, the National Security Advisory Group, with such notable participants as William J. Perry, Madaleine K. Albright, Wesley K. Clark, John D. Podesta, and John M. Shalikashvili, published a report entitled, "The U.S. Military: Under Strain and at Risk." In this report provided to the Senate, they contend that, "while the U.S. military has performed superbly in Afghanistan, Iraq and elsewhere, our ground forces are under enormous strain. This strain, if not soon relieved, will have highly corrosive and potentially long-term effects on the force."[283]

Conclusion

In retrospect in many ways, it appears that while much has changed in the 50-plus years since the Korean War, we're in a time and a place where possibly some of the reasons for which we did not use nuclear weapons in the 1950's, may in fact still apply in this particular scenario today. After laying out ideas as to why this country did not use WMD during the Korean War in an attempt to win, or at least conclude the conflict on a more favorable footing for the U.S, and then analyzing those same issues under today's microscope, I contend that the U.S administration would choose not to retaliate through the use of nuclear weapons. Before going any farther, I believe it is imperative to reiterate the underlying premise of this research paper. The scenario in which I chose to use, dealt with a surprise North Korean missile attack which was successfully thwarted by U.S. defensive systems with no resulting damage. In fact, other than for satellite launch reports and radar data, there exists no tangible evidence that the attack ever actually occurred.

I believe the U.S. would not resort to the use of nuclear weapons in this situation for these two primary reasons: the "just war tradition" and its inherent tenants of maintaining the moral high ground and that of proportionality. For reasons I've already touched upon earlier, I contend that the administration would come to the conclusion that our use of nuclear weapons in retaliation would negate our moral high ground, and that serious questions would arise dealing with proportionality—especially when our TV screens, and those around the world, became flooded with sickening pictures of the devastation wrought by a single U.S. nuclear retaliatory strike—especially when the same devastation was not evident on U.S. soil.

Secondly, and as a natural follow-on to the first, is that if the President and administration chose to use the military arm of our national power, there are other viable, and equally effective means of achieving the desired effect and objectives—whatever those happen to be. Whether it is regime change or a reduction of North Korea's military strength, the U.S. has other weapons within its arsenal to achieve those ends, as is substantiated in the earlier cited RAND study—without resorting to WMD. With the proliferation of precision guided munitions and their significant capabilities, there are more than enough recent case studies including Desert Storm (Gulf War I), Operation Deliberate Force (Kosovo Campaign), Operation Enduring Freedom and now most recently Operation Iraqi Freedom that show it is very possible to achieve our military aims without resorting to letting the proverbial "genie out of the bottle" once again.

Thus, I believe that Kim Jong-il and North Korea would not have the dubious distinction of becoming the second nation to experience the wrath of atomic detonations in anger upon their soil.

I will end this paper in much the same way that I started. Ironically, this answer is exactly what then-President Reagan had in mind in 1983 when he uttered these words,

> What if free people could live secure in the knowledge that their security did not rest upon the threat of instant US retaliation to deter a Soviet attack, that we could intercept and destroy strategic ballistic missiles before they reached our own soil or that of our allies? I know this is a formidable, technical task, one that may not be accomplished before the end of this century. Yet, current technology has attained a level of sophistication where it's reasonable for us to begin this effort. It will take years, probably decades of effort on many fronts. There will be failures and setbacks, just as there will be successes and breakthroughs. And as we proceed, we must remain constant in preserving the nuclear deterrent and maintaining a solid capability for flexible response. But isn't it worth every investment necessary to free the world from the threat of nuclear war? We know it is.[284]

If I am correct, then we have just moved a step farther away from nuclear retaliation. The late President Reagan would be smiling at such a possibility.

Endnotes

[1] Missile Defense Agency, *A Historic Beginning, BMDS Booklet Second Edition* (Washington DC, 2003), 2.

[2] U.S Congress, Senate Armed Services Committee, Strategic Forces Subcommittee, *Missile Defense Program and Fiscal Year 2006 Budget,* 109 Congress, 7 April 2005, 3.

[3] Hearing of the Strategic Forces Subcommittee of the House Armed Services Committee, available from http://web.lexis-nexis.com/universe/document?_m=e15a0e43c6c6860b46; Internet; accessed 1 December 2005.

[4] Ibid., 3.

[5] "North Korea Boasts of the Bomb, But Can it Deliver?" NSSI Newsletter, (30 November 2005): 10.

[6] Ibid.

[7] Ibid.

[8] Mark W. Clark, From the Danube to the Yalu (New York, New York. Harper & Brothers Publishers, 1954), 1.

[9] Michio Kaku and Daniel Axelrod, To Win A Nuclear War: The Pentagon's Secret War Plans (Boston, MA: South End Press, Year), 44.

[10] Ibid.

[11] Samual R. Williamson, Jr. and Steven L. Reardon, The Origins of U.S. Nuclear Strategy, 1945-1953 (New York, New York, Publisher, 1993) 145.

[12] Steven T. Ross, American War Plans 1945-1950 (New York, New York: Garland Publishing, Inc., 1988) 12.

[13] James L. Stokesbury, A Short History of the Korean War (New York, New York: William Morrow, 1988), 40.

[14] Kaku, 44.

[15] David Allen Rosenberg, "US Nuclear Stockpile, 1945-1950," The Bulletin of the Atomic Scientists, May 1982, 29.

[16] Ibid.

[17] Ross, 14.

[18] Ibid.

[19] Ibid.

[20] Kaku, 43.

[21] Ibid.

[22] Williamson, 101.

[23] Ibid.

[24] Ibid, 102.

[25] Ibid.

[26] Ibid, 104.

[27] Ibid, 107.

[28] Ibid.

[29] Ibid.

[30] Daniel Calingaert, "Nuclear Weapons and the Korean War" *Journal of Strategic Studies*, no. 11 (June 1988) 188.

[31] Ross, 138-140.

[32] Ibid.

[33] Williamson, 124.

[34] Paul G. Peirpaoli, *Truman and Korea—The Political Culture of the Early Cold War* (Missouri: Publishers, 1999), 26.

[35] Ibid.

[36] Ibid.

[37] Morton Halperin, *Limited War in the Nuclear Age* (New York: Wiley, 1963), 40.

[38] Max Hastings, *The Korean War* (New York: Simon & Schuster, 1987), 186.

[39] Halperin, 39.

[40] Daniel Calingaert, "Nuclear Weapons and the Korean War" *Journal of Strategic Studies*, no. 11 (June 1988) 183.

[41] Ibid, 183.

[42] David Allen Rosenberg, "US Nuclear Stockpile, 1945-1950," *The Bulletin of the Atomic Scientists,* May 1982, 26.

[43] Ibid.

[44] Ibid.

[45] Calingaert, 184.

[46] Ibid.

[47] Brookings Betts, *Nuclear Blackmail and Nuclear Balance* (Washington DC: Brookings Institution, 1987), 32.

[48] Ibid.

[49] Roger Dingman, "Atomic Diplomacy During the Korean War," *International Security,* no. 13 (Winter '88-'89): 56.

[50] Ibid.

[51] Callum A. MacDonald, *Korea: The War Before Vietnam* (New York: Macmillan, 1986), 38.

[52] Ibid.

[53] Ibid.

[54] Ibid.

[55] Samual R. Williamson, Jr. and Steven L. Reardon, *The Origins of U.S. Nuclear Strategy, 1945-1953* (New York, New York, Publisher, 1993) 139-140.

[56] Ibid.

[57] Moody, 345-347.

[58] Ibid.

[59] Ibid.

[60] Clay Blair, *The Forgotten War: America in Korea 1950-1953* (New York: Times Books, 1987), 78.

[61] Ibid.

[62] Ibid.

[63] D. Clayton James, *The Years of MacArthur Volume III 1945-1964* (Boston: Houghton Mifflin Company, 1985), 578.

[64] Dingman, 62.

[65] Ibid.

[66] Blair, 124.

[67] Ibid.

[68] MacDonald, 39.

[69] Ibid.

[70] Ibid.

[71] Calingaert, 185.

[72] James, 581.

[73] Dingman, 60-62.

[74] Ibid.

[75] James, 578-579.

[76] Ibid.

[77] MacDonald, 39.

[78] Ibid.

[79] Calingeart, 185.

[80] Ibid.

[81] Ibid.

[82] Moody, 355.

[83] Ibid.

[84] Bevin Alexander, *Korea: The First War We Lost* (New York: Hippocrene Books, 1986), 47.

[85] Ibid.

[86] Ibid.

[87] Ibid.

[88] Ibid.

[89] Ibid.

[90] Ibid.

[91] Dingman, 61.

[92] Ibid.

[93] Insidor F. Stone, *The Hidden History of the Korean War* (New York: Monthly Review Press, 1952), 245.

[94] Ibid.

[95] Ibid.

[96] Ibid.

[97] Ibid.

[98] Ibid.

[99] Ibid.

[100] Ibid.

[101] Blair, 526.

[102] Ibid.

[103] Ibid.

[104] Ibid.

[105] Ibid.

[106] Ibid.

[107] Ibid, 527.

[108] Ibid.

[109] Ibid.

[110] Ibid.

[111] William T. Y'Blood, *The Three Wars of Lt Gen George E. Stratemeyer: His Korean War Diary* (Washington DC: Air Force History & Museums Program, 1999) 322. MacDonald, 71.

[112] Michio Kaku and Daniel Axelrod, *To Win A Nuclear War: The Pentagon's Secret War Plans* (Boston, MA: South End Press, Year), 72

[113] Ibid.

[114] Ibid.

[115] Betts, 33.

[116] Ibid.

[117] Blair, 523.

[118] Ibid.

[119] Ibid.

[120] Joint Chiefs of Staff, *The Joint Chiefs of Staff and National Policy Volume III 1950-1951, The Korean War: Part One* (Washington: 1998), 155.

[121] Dingman, 67.

[122] Ibid.

[123] Y'Blood, 321.

[124] Kaku, 72.

[125] Ibid.

[126] Ibid.

[127] Ibid.

[128] Moody, 350.

[129] Ibid.

[130] Ibid.

[131] Hastings, 183-184.

[132] Ibid.

[133] Ibid.

[134] Matthew Ridgeway, *The Korean War* (Garden City New York: Doubleday, 1967), 76.

[135] Robert Futrell, *The United States Air Force in Korea, 1950-1953* (Washington: Office of Air Force History, 1983), 241.

[136] Michio Kaku and Daniel Axelrod, *To Win A Nuclear War: The Pentagon's Secret War Plans* (Boston, MA: South End Press, Year), 72.

[137] Ibid.

[138] Ibid.

[139] Ibid.

[140] Conrad C. Crane, "Raiding the Beggar's Pantry: The Search for Airpower Strategy in the Korean War," *Journal of Military History,* no. 63 (October 1999): 896.

[141] Ibid.

[142] Joint Chiefs of Staff, *The Joint Chiefs of Staff and National Policy Volume III 1950-1951, The Korean War: Part Two* (Washington: 1998), 27.

[143] Ibid.

[144] Joint Chiefs of Staff, Part Two, 27.

[145] Ibid., 28.

[146] Brookings Betts, *Nuclear Blackmail and Nuclear Balance* (Washington DC: Brookings Institution, 1987), 35.

[147] Crane, 902.

[148] Roger Dingman, "Atomic Diplomacy During the Korean War," *International Security,* no. 13 (Winter '88-'89): 69-73.

[149] Ibid.

[150] Crane, 902.

[151] Ibid.

[152] Ibid.

[153] Dingman, 73.

[154] Ibid., 77.

[155] Ibid.

[156] Ibid., 76.

[157] Ibid, 76-78.

[158] Ibid.

[159] Ibid., 77.

[160] Insidor F. Stone, *The Hidden History of the Korean War* (New York: Monthly Review Press, 1952), 282.

[161] Ibid.

[162] Joint Chiefs of Staff, Part Two, 56.

[163] Clay Blair, *The Forgotten War: America in Korea 1950 1953* (New York: Times Books, 1987), 653.

[164] Ibid.

[165] Daniel Calingaert, "Nuclear Weapons and the Korean War" *Journal of Strategic Studies*, no. 11 (June 1988) 185.

[166] Ibid.

[167] Ibid.

[168] Ibid.

[169] Ridgeway, 76.

[170] Betts, 36. Crane, 903. Callum A. MacDonald, *Korea: The War Before Vietnam* (New York: Macmillan, 1986), 132.

[171] Calingaert, 188.

[172] Betts, 36.

[173] Crane, 903.

[174] Ibid.

[175] MacDonald, 132.

[176] Bruce Kennedy, "The Moscow Connection," *CNN Cold War,* 4; on-line, Internet, 14 February 2000, available from http://www.cnn.com/SPECIALS/cold.war/episodes/05/spotlight/.

[177] Brookings Betts, *Nuclear Blackmail and Nuclear Balance* (Washington DC: Brookings Institution, 1987), 36.

[178] Callum A. MacDonald, *Korea: The War Before Vietnam* (New York: Macmillan, 1986), 168.

[179] Ibid.

[180] Joint Chiefs of Staff, Part Two, 192. Bevin Alexander, *Korea: The First War We Lost* (New York: Hippocrene Books, 1986), 468.

[181] Bevin Alexander, *Korea: The First War We Lost* (New York: Hippocrene Books, 1986), 468.

[182] Ibid.

[183] Ibid.

[184] Ibid.

[185] Ibid.

[186] MacDonald, 175.

[187] Joint Chiefs of Staff, Part Two, 193.

[188] Mark W. Clark, *From the Danube to the Yalu* (New York, New York. Harper & Brothers Publishers, 1954), 3.

[189] Joint Chiefs of Staff, Part Two, 193.

[190] Rosemary Foot, "Nuclear Coercion and the Ending of the Korean Conflict," *International Security,* no. 13 (Winter '88-'89): 94.

[191] Ibid.

[192] Betts, 37.

[193] Edward Keefer, "President Dwight D. Eisenhower and the End of the Korean War," *International Security,* no. 10 (Summer '86) 270.

[194] Ibid.

[195] Dingman, 82.

[196] Callum A. MacDonald, *Korea: The War Before Vietnam* (New York: Macmillan, 1986), 177.

[197] Ibid.

[198] Ibid.

[199] Edward Keefer, "President Dwight D. Eisenhower and the End of the Korean War," *International Security,* no. 10 (Summer '86) 271-277.

[200] Daniel Calingaert, "Nuclear Weapons and the Korean War" *Journal of Strategic Studies*, no. 11 (June 1988) 184.

[201] Ibid.

[202] Ibid.

[203] Ibid.

[204] Ibid.

[205] William T. Y'Blood, *The Three Wars of Lt Gen George E. Stratemeyer: His Korean War Diary* (Boston, MA: 1972) 342.

[206] Ibid.

[207] Michio Kaku and Daniel Axelrod, *To Win A Nuclear War: The Pentagon's Secret War Plans* (Boston, MA: South End Press, 1987), 82.

[208] Ibid.

[209] Keefer, 277.

[210] Kaku, 80.

[211] Keefer, 268.

[212] Kaku, 80.

[213] Brookings Betts, *Nuclear Blackmail and Nuclear Balance* (Washington DC: Brookings Institution, 1987), 38.

[214] Kaku, 82.

[215] Ibid.

[216] Ibid.

[217] Keefer, 272.

[218] Ibid.

[219] Joint Chiefs of Staff, Part Two, 203.

[220] Joint Chiefs of Staff, Part Two, 207.

[221] Ibid.

[222] Ibid.

[223] Calingaert, 194.

[224] Kaku, 81.

[225] Rosemary Foot, "Nuclear Coercion and the Ending of the Korean Conflict," *International Security,* no. 13 (Winter '88-'89): 98.

[226] Ibid.

[227] Ibid.

[228] Ibid.

[229] Ibid.

[230] Kaku, 2. MacDonald, 177.

[231] Keefer, 278.

[232] Ibid.

[233] Ibid, 279-280.

[234] Ibid., 268.

[235] Ibid.

[236] Ibid.

[237] Ibid, 268-281.

[238] Ibid, 269.

[239] Ibid, 276.

[240] Ibid.

[241] Ibid.

[242] Ibid, 277.

[243] Calingaert, 194.

[244] Ibid.

[245] Joint Chiefs of Staff, *The Joint Chiefs of Staff and National Policy Volume III 1951-1953, The Korean War: Part Two* (Washington: 1998), 207.

[246] Daniel Calingaert, "Nuclear Weapons and the Korean War" *Journal of Strategic Studies*, no. 11 (June 1988) 194-197.

[247] Callum A. MacDonald, *Korea: The War Before Vietnam* (New York: Macmillan, 1986), 179.

[248] Morton Halperin, *Limited War in the Nuclear Age* (New York: Wiley, 1963), 40.

[249] Ibid.

[250] Ibid,43.

[251] Ibid.

[252] Ibid.

[253] Robert Futrell, *The United States Air Force in Korea, 1950-1953* (Washington: Office of Air Force History, 1983), 241.

[254] Walton S. Moody, *Building A Strategic Air Force* (Air Force History and Museums Program: US Government Printing Office, 1990), 386.

[255] Barton J. Bernstein, "Truman and the A-Bomb: Targeting Noncombatants, Using the Bomb, and His Defending the 'Decision,'" *Journal of Military History* 62, nos. 3-4 (Jul-Oct 1998): 547.

[256] Admiral Stansfield Turner, "The Dilemma of Nuclear Weapons in the Twenty-First Century," *NWC Review* (Spring 2001): available from http://www.nwc.navy.mil/press/ Review/2001Spring/art1-sp1.htm; Internet; accessed 15 February 2006.

[257] Center for Nonproliferation Studies, "New Nuclear Weapons?" available from http://www.cns.miis.edu/pubs/week/030528.htm

[258] Los Alamos National Laboratory, "Los Alamos restores U.S. ability to make nuclear weapons," available from http://www.lanl.gov/news/releases/archive/03-054.shtml

[259] Glenn C. Buchan et al., *Future Roles of U.S. Nuclear Forces* (Santa Monica, CA: RAND, 2003), iii.

[260] Ibid.,48.

[261] Ibid., 58, 61, 63.

[262] Ibid., 57.

[263] Ibid., 58.

[264] Ibid., 69.

[265] Jill Marie Parillo, "Nouveaute in Nuclear Deterrence," available from http://www.carnegieendowment.org/publications/index.cfm?fa=print&id=18052; Internet; accessed 1 March 2006.

[266] John Pike, "Nuclear Threats During the Gulf War," 19 February 1998; available from http://www.fas.org/irp/eprint/ds-threats.htm; Internet; accessed 2 March 2006.

[267] Ibid.

[268] Ian Smith, "Bush: Nuke 'Em; Leaked US Papers Vow to Use Nuclear Weapons on Iraq," *Scottish Daily Record & Sunday Mail Ltd,* 1 February 2003, p. 13.

[269] George Farebrother, "Nuclear Weapons, Uncertainty and the Law," available from http://www.russfound.org/Launch/farebrother1.htm; Internet; accessed 2 March 2006.

[270] Edward F. Bruner, *North Korean Crisis: Possible Military Options (Congressional Research Service: The Library of Congress, 2003), 6.*

[271] Buchan, 21.

[272] Ellen Tausher, "Cold War Comeback? The nuclear threat from within," 18 November 2003; available from http://www.house.gov/tauscher/issues/op-ed-nuclearweapons-11-18-03.html; Internet; accessed 8 November 2005.

[273] C. Paul Robinson, "A White Paper: Pursuing a New Nuclear Weapons Policy for the 21 st Century," 22 March 2001; available from http://www.sandia.gov/media/whitepaper/2001-04-Robinson.htm; Internet; accessed 8 November 2005.

[274] Buchan, 6.

[275] Turner, 9.

[276] Joseph R. Biden, Jr., "Don't Raze the Nuclear 'Firewall,'" 16 May 2002; available from http://www.biden.senate.giv/newsroom/details.cfm?id=182789&&; Internet; accessed 8 November 2005.

[277] Barry Zellen, "Rethinking the Unthinkable: Nuclear Weapons and the War on Terror," *Strategic Insights,* January 2004; available from http://www.ccc.nps.navy.mil/si/2004/jan/ zellenJan04.asp; Internet; accessed 8 November 2005.

[278] Robert G. Spulak, "The Case in Favor of US Nuclear Weapons," *Parameters, US Army War College Quarterly,* Spring 1997; available from http://carlisle-www.army.mil/usawc/ Parameters/97spring/spulak.htm; Internet; accessed 8 November 2005.

[279] Conrad C. Crane, "Raiding the Beggar's Pantry: The Search for Airpower Strategy in the Korean War," *Journal of Military History,* no. 63 (October 1999): 890. Halperin, 46.

[280] Dr Harry Yarger, "Policy and Strategy Formulation Process," lecture, U.S. Army War College, Carlisle Barracks, PA, 28 October 2005.

[281] Buchan, 96.

[282] Bruner, 6.

[283] William J. Perry, "The U.S. Military: Under Strain and at Risk," January 2006; available from http://www.senate.gov/~reed/documents/Reports/National%20Security%20Report% 2001252006.pdf; Internet; accessed 2 March 2006.

[284] Missile Defense Agency, *A Historic Beginning, BMDS Booklet Second Edition* (Washington DC, 2003), 2.

www.ingramcontent.com/pod-product-compliance
Lightning Source LLC
Chambersburg PA
CBHW081330310526
45789CB00018B/2830